E
YA.

melt

100

AMAZING ADVENTURES

in Grilled Cheese

Shane (Sanford) Kearns *Creator, GrilledShane.com*

Aadamsmedia

Avon, Massachusetts

Published by
Adams Media, a division of F+W Media, Inc.
57 Littlefield Street, Avon, MA 02322. U.S.A.
www.adamsmedia.com
ISBN 10: 1-4405-3874-3
ISBN 13: 978-1-4405-3874-2
eISBN 10: 1-4405-4291-0
eISBN 13: 978-1-4405-4291-6

Printed in China.

10 9 8 7 6 5 4 3 2 1

Library of Congress Cataloging-in-Publication Data
Kearns, Shane.
Melt / Shane Kearns.
p. cm.
Includes index.
ISBN 978-1-4405-3874-2 (paper over board) – ISBN 1-4405-3874-3 (paper over board) – ISBN 978-1-4405-4291-6
(ebook) – ISBN 1-4405-4291-0 (ebook)
1. Sandwiches. 2. Cooking (Cheese) 3. Skillet cooking. I. Title.
TX818.K43 2012
641.84–dc23
2012014509

Always follow safety and commonsense cooking protocol while using kitchen utensils, operating ovens and stoves, and handling uncooked food. If children are assisting in the preparation of any recipe, they should always be supervised by an adult.

This publication is designed to provide accurate and authoritative information with regard to the subject matter covered. It is sold with the understanding that the publisher is not engaged in rendering legal, accounting, or other professional advice. If legal advice or other expert assistance is required, the services of a competent professional person should be sought.

—From a *Declaration of Principles* jointly adopted by a Committee of
the American Bar Association and a Committee of Publishers and Associations

Photos courtesy of Shane (Sanford) Kearns. Photos on pages 67 and 92 Stephanie Chrusz.

This book is available at quantity discounts for bulk purchases.
For information, please call 1-800-289-0963.

Dedication

For my mother . . . it's as simple as that.

Acknowledgments

Everyone remembers the first time they sank their teeth into a toasted white bread traditional grilled cheese. This experience is enhanced by the memory of this grilled cheese cooked with love by their mother or grandmother. It is a memory that I have cherished of my Nanny and mom. It is a memory that has moved me to create this cookbook and to share my passion for a grilled cheese sandwich with the world.

There are many people I would like to acknowledge for making this cookbook a reality. My family, first and foremost, was truly there for me during the entire process. My father was always there with an empty stomach and a knife and fork, willing to taste any sandwich I created. My sister Jaime and brother-in-law Adam answered my business questions and always took an interest. My two nephews, Nathan and Andrew, provided me with inspiration to create two grilled cheese sandwiches based on their favorite meals. Nate inspired "Stuffed French Toast," also known as French Toast Cookies, while Drew's recent diagnosis of Celiac disease and new diet drove me to create "The Snack Time," or Drewliscious.

Located in small-town Ohio, my great-aunt Betty, surprised by most of the ingredients included in this cookbook, always asked, "What sandwich are you creating today?"

Occasionally, as I was cooking, I would run out of an ingredient. Thankfully, my neighbors, Susan and Roger, were there to lend a helping hand with extras from their pantry.

Without the understanding of my boss, Kori, I would not have had the opportunity to enjoy the creation of this book. Thank you.

Ingredients mentioned in this book were purchased at local mainstays Miles Farmers Market and Heinen's as well as Whole Foods Market and Giant Eagle. The Cheese Lady from Miles and Cheesemonger Jason, from Whole Foods, were instrumental with creative suggestions.

Finally, I must thank my good friend Kyle for creating the moniker "GrilledShane." Without his quick creativity, I might still be trying to develop my grilled cheese identity.

Contents

Introduction 9
*How to Rock a Reimagined
Grilled Cheese* 10

Part 1
*Seriously Savory
Sandwiches* 13

Chapter 1
*Gastronomically
Gourmet* 14

Balsamic Basil 15
Basil Peppercorn 16
Pistachio and Beets 19
Classic Meatballs Marinara 20
Fusion Salmon Piccata 21
Ahi Tuna Steak Melt 22
Curried Egg Salad 23
The Updated Caprese 24
Soup-less French Onion 26
The Mediterranean 27
Prosciutto and Arugula 28

Roasted Brussels Sprouts with
    Cheddar .29
Crème Fraîche with Apple and
    Cucumber 31
The Blue Potato 32
Quinoa Black Bean 33
The Sunday Brunch 34
Sunflower Gouda Griller 36
White Wine and Mushrooms 37
BBQ Chickpeas 38
Roasted Garlic Tomato Aioli 39
Ciliegine with Lime Vinaigrette 41
The Spicy Soy 42
Tillamook Cheddar and Baby Bok Choy . . .43
Cayenne Cornbread 44
The Fried Egg 46
The Bacon Filet 47
Salmon Croquettes with Dill 49
Asparagus and Lemon Pepper
    Vinaigrette 50
Homemade Salsa 52

Chapter 2
Living on the Edge 53

The Deconstructed. 54

Sweet and Spicy Popcorn 55

Veggies and Dip 56

The Unusual Reuben 57

Fish 'N Chips 58

Sea Salt Hummus 60

Green Tea Tofu. 61

The Ramen 63

The Beer, Kale, and Crouton Mash-Up. 64

The Wedgie 65

Risotto 66

The Double Decker 68

Broccoli Alfredo. 69

Stuffed Mushrooms 71

Oh! Rings 72

Farfalle Pesto Grilled Cheese 75

Stuffed Chips 76

Inside-Out Blue Cheese Pecan 77

The Savory Waffle 78

Ultimate Cheesy Fries 81

Pretzel Baked Beans. 82

The Scrambled Spanakopita 85

The Pizza Volcano. 86

Boneless Buffalo Wings 87

The Hashbrown 88

Fried Matzoh with Horseradish Mayo 90

Garlic and Green Onion Mashed Potato . . .91

The Potato Pancake 93

The Spicy Dubliner 94

Mini-Eggplant Sliders 97

Big Game Nachos and Cheese 98

Part 2
Surprisingly Sweet Stacks *99*

Chapter 3
Epicurean Adventures 100

The Nutella. 101

Harvest Fest 102

Honey Roasted PB & J. 104

Squash with Apple Butter. 105

Marinated Berries 106

Coconut Peach 108

Kicked-Up Mint 109

The Tropical 111

Currant Jam 112

Walnut Pomegranate 113

Apple Pie 114

Pineapple Brown Butter 116

Cinnamon Kiwi. 117

Carrot Cake 118

Boston Cream Pie. 121

The Granola Bar. 122

Sweet Grapes and Brie 123

Chocolate Mascarpone and Strawberry . .124

Strawberry-Mango. 126

Mascarpone Pound Cake. 145

Cherries Jubilee 146

Amaretto Rhubarb 148

The Snack Time 149

Crunchy Chocolate Peanut 150

The Twisted Parfait 151

Sea Salt Caramel 152

Pumpkin Pie. 153

The Candy Cane 154

Chapter 4
Experimental Territory 127

Dessert Waffles 128

Cheerios and Honey 129

Stuffed French Toast. 131

The Candied Baconator 132

Rice Krispies Treats 133

Coffee Sponge Cake 134

The S'more 135

Chocolate Brownie Indulgence 136

Crème de Menthe 138

Noodle Pudding. 139

The Cinnamon Roll. 141

Cookie Cheesecake. 142

Appendix
Suitable Substitutions 156

Index. 158

Introduction

Do you remember the first time you slowly sank your teeth into a gooey grilled cheese? Maybe you were home from school on a snow day or enjoying a weekend spent with your mom or dad. Your sandwich was probably made with white bread, American cheese, and a little bit of butter—delicious!

You may not be a child anymore, but here's some great news: The traditional grilled cheese sandwich has grown up with you! Today's grilled cheese sandwiches are filled with out-of-this world ingredients that take the humble grilled cheese to a whole new level. Looking for a savory sandwich? In Part 1 you'll find grilled cheeses packed full of amazing ingredients like quinoa, blue cheese, eggplant, and even green onion mashed potatoes. And if you're looking for a sandwich to sweeten the pot, you'll find it in Part 2, where ingredients like pomegranate, brie, bacon, and sea salt caramel reign supreme!

Whether you're a meat lover, a veggie lover, or a lover of anything ooey, gooey, and in-your-face amazing, the flavor-packed grilled cheese sandwiches found throughout this book will give you what you're looking for in a big way!

Grilled cheese's time has arrived—and so has yours! Enjoy!

How to Rock a Reimagined Grilled Cheese

When you first think of cooking grilled cheese sandwiches, you may picture only the basics: Smear butter over each slice of bread, throw a slice of cheese in there, and voilà. But even though creating a truly amazing grilled cheese isn't hard, here you will find special steps to make your grilled cheese even more impressive.

MELT

Here are two mistakes people make. Some folks just smear on the butter, which causes the bread to fall apart and creates an unevenly cooked sandwich. Others melt the butter in the sauté pan and then plop in the bread and filling, which won't create the crunchy, golden brown bread that is synonymous with the grilled cheese sandwich. Instead, you should always melt the butter first and then spread it on the outsides of both slices of your desired bread before it even touches the pan. This will ensure that the bread cooks evenly and will provide that much-loved crunchy texture that really makes a grilled cheese something special.

Note: *All sandwiches in this cookbook were created with Land O'Lakes Salted Whipped Butter found in a tub, an ingredient that has withstood the test of time through many generations of kitchen use.*

SAVOR THE FLAVOR

Let's be honest: There are a lot of different types of cheeses out there, some of which you may not even have heard about or gotten up the courage to try. But when you try different types of cheeses, you increase the odds of taking your sandwiches from run-of-the-mill to remarkable. Be adventurous and try something new. Your taste buds will thank you.

Cheddar cheese is one of the most popular cheeses in the world, but you may not have tried its alter ego, sharp Cheddar. In most instances, sharp Cheddar provides more bite and overall flavor than mild Cheddar and will help you create a much better grilled cheese sandwich. If you're hesitant, just give sharp Cheddar one try; you'll likely become a believer. But if it's just too much for your taste buds, simply replace sharp Cheddar with your favorite variety of Cheddar in the recipes throughout.

Dessert cheeses, such as mascarpone or crème fraîche, are limited in number and may be intimidating if you haven't really worked with them before. The dessert cheeses' differences in texture and flavor profiles are small but their uses are many. Some are thick and chunky while others are runny and need a delicate touch when spreading on a grilled cheese. Ease your way into the world of dessert grilled cheeses by trying out some of the recipes in Part 2. Then take things to the next level and use these cheeses to create your own unique, dessert grilled cheese sandwiches.

If you're at the supermarket and you're not sure what brands of cheese to buy, don't get overwhelmed. Some favorites include Mackenzie Creamery, Kerrygold, Barber's 1833, Tillamook, Cabot, and Cowgirl Creamery.

Note: *Cheese is available in all different forms, which makes it hard to tell you exactly how cheese should be handled. However, in most situations, sliced cheeses do not melt evenly and may cause your hoped-for perfect grilled cheese to fall a bit short. To get around this meltdown—or lack thereof—it is important to shred the desired cheese prior to cooking, which allows for more even melting and an amazing sandwich.*

BRING THE HEAT

The best way to cook up an over-the-top, ooey, gooey grilled cheese is to use a nonstick sauté pan, which leaves the bread crunchy and the cheese perfectly melted. Other options, such as a sandwich press, cast iron pan, or even a grill, are all great and valid choices, but the nonstick pan outperforms the rest. Use it and use it often.

HAVE SOME FUN

When it comes right down to it, each and every person is capable of putting a unique spin on a grilled cheese sandwich with those little touches that make a sandwich personal and special. In this cookbook, you'll find some pretty amazing—and inventive—grilled cheese sandwiches, but don't stop here. Take this knowledge and run with it to create unique sandwiches that are so unreal that they haven't even been thought of yet. And if you're not feeling all that imaginative—or if you can't find the breads or cheeses called for in the recipes in the stores—don't worry about it! Check out the substitution appendix at the back of the book. Your grilled cheese will always reign supreme—and you won't regret a bit of it.

Long live the grilled cheese!

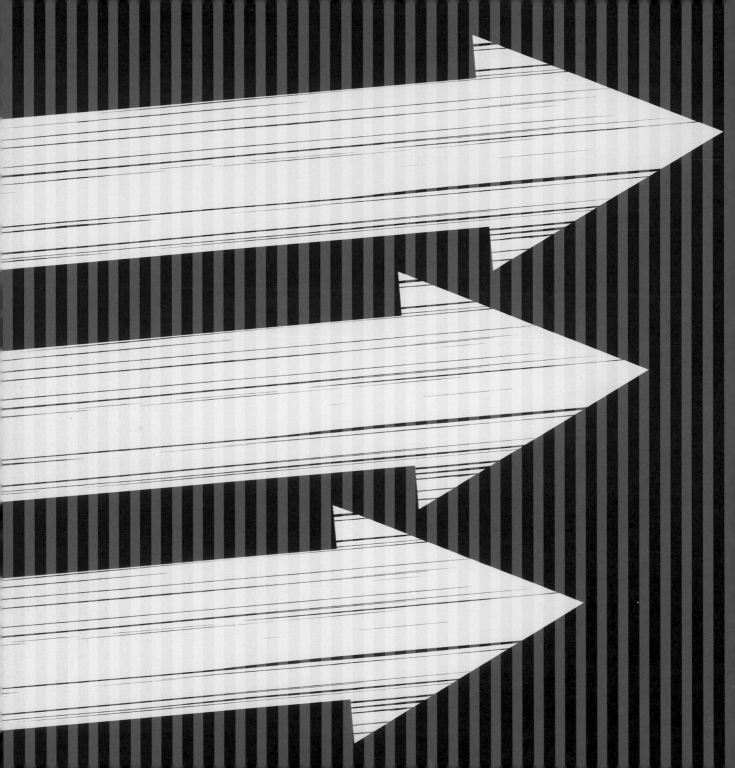

Part 1

Seriously Savory Sandwiches

Crème Fraîche with Apple and Cucumber. Sweet and Spicy Popcorn. The Beer, Kale, and Crouton Mash-Up.

No matter their names, the savory grilled cheeses found in this part run the gamut from unexpectedly unreal to blissfully bizarre. The gourmet sandwiches in Chapter 1 kick tradition up a notch with sophisticated ingredients like lime vinaigrette, freshly cracked black pepper, filet mignon, and white wine, while the edgy stacks in Chapter 2 toe the line with ingredients like green tea, buffalo wings, tofu, and ramen noodles. And while bread seems like an integral part of a sandwich, here you'll learn how to push the envelope and replace this staple with ingredients such as eggplant or portobello mushrooms. The possibilities end only when your imagination does.

Chapter 1

Gastronomically Gourmet

Americans may have been raised on grilled cheese sandwiches best described as traditional, but grilled cheese doesn't have to be limited to white bread and plastic-wrapped cheese squares. With the explosion of culinary interest, the grilled cheese sandwich has been given a gourmet status. The ingredients, breads, and cheeses have all evolved. Now, instead of white bread, sourdough, whole wheat/multigrain, and pita are stealing the show. American cheese has been replaced by sharp Cheddar, smoked Gouda, or goat cheese. Standard "extras" like tomatoes and onions are now heirloom and caramelized. So head to your local farmers' market or supermarket and see what a little gourmet can give you!

Balsamic Basil

½ cup Hellmann's mayonnaise

¼ cup fresh basil, finely minced

1 tablespoon balsamic vinegar, divided

1 cup cauliflower

2–4 tablespoons melted sweet butter, for grilling

2 slices honey whole wheat bread

½ cup shredded sharp Cheddar cheese

In this recipe, the creamy mayonnaise and the smooth cauliflower combine to create a flawless flavor base. But if you're afraid that this sandwich might be too one-note, think again! The sharp Cheddar cheese bites through all this creaminess and creates a unique flavor profile that gets the job done!

❶ "Steam" the cauliflower in the microwave by placing them in a microwave-safe bowl with enough water to cover the bottom of the bowl. Cover and cook on high for 30 seconds.

❷ In a small mixing bowl, combine mayonnaise, fresh basil, and ¾ tablespoon balsamic vinegar. In a separate bowl, combine remaining ¼ tablespoon balsamic vinegar and cauliflower.

❸ Brush the melted butter on the outside of the 2 slices of bread. In an unheated sauté pan, place 1 slice of bread butter side down. Spread the balsamic basil mayonnaise on the bread followed by the cauliflower and sharp Cheddar cheese. Place other slice of bread on top, butter side up. Turn burner to medium heat.

❹ Let sandwich cook for 3–5 minutes per side or until bread is golden brown.

❺ Cut on the diagonal and serve warm.

Basil Peppercorn

Serves 1

⅛ cup sliced Vidalia onions, caramelized

1 tablespoon fresh basil, chopped

⅛ cup + 1 tablespoon whole peppercorns

1 tablespoon water

¼ pound chunk Chaumes cheese

2 slices Italian bread

2–4 tablespoons melted sweet butter, for grilling

¼ cup shredded Havarti cheese

Caramelizing the Vidalia onions found in this recipe brings out their natural sweetness and adds a sophisticated flavor to this upscale grilled cheese. To caramelize onions, melt 2 tablespoons sweet butter in a sauté pan. Add half of a Vidalia onion, sliced, and cook on medium heat, stirring occasionally. Cook until onions begin to brown and set aside, approximately 10–12 minutes. Make sure not to burn.

❶ Combine basil, whole peppercorns, and water in a blender until mixed to a powder-like substance. Thoroughly knead the peppercorn mixture into the Chaumes cheese by hand and set aside.

❷ Brush 2–4 tablespoons melted butter on the outside of the 2 slices of bread. In an unheated sauté pan, place 1 slice of bread butter side down. Sprinkle shredded Havarti on the bread, followed by peppercorn mixture and caramelized onions. Place the other slice of bread on top, butter side up. Turn burner to medium heat.

❸ Let sandwich cook on medium heat for 3–5 minutes per side or until bread is golden brown.

❹ Cut on the diagonal and serve warm.

Pistachio and Beets

Pistachio and Beets

Serves 1

If you're looking for a grilled cheese sandwich with a little style, then this one is right up your alley! The bright colors of the green pistachios and red beets swirl together in a melty mix of provolone cheese. Bet you can't eat just one!

2–4 tablespoons melted sweet butter, for grilling

2 slices honey whole wheat bread

4 slices canned beets

4–5 pieces marinated artichokes

⅛ cup shelled, salted pistachios, halved

½ cup shredded provolone cheese

Dried thyme, to taste

❶ Brush the melted butter on the outside of the 2 slices of bread. In an unheated sauté pan, place 1 slice of bread butter side down.

❷ Place beets, artichoke pieces, pistachios, and shredded provolone cheese on top. Sprinkle dried thyme to taste. Place other slice of bread on top, butter side up. Turn burner to medium heat.

❸ Let sandwich cook for 3–5 minutes per side or until bread is golden brown.

❹ Cut on the diagonal and serve warm.

Classic Meatballs Marinara

This grown-up meatball sub is a guest recipe that takes humble cafeteria fare and amps it up to a true gourmet treat. Enjoy!

FOR MEATBALLS

1 pound ground beef

1 clove garlic, minced

1 egg

½ cup freshly grated Romano cheese

2¼ teaspoons chopped Italian flat leaf parsley

1 teaspoon salt

¾ cup Italian bread crumbs

⅔ cup milk

½ cup olive oil or vegetable oil, for frying

¼ cup store-bought marinara sauce

FOR SANDWICH

2 slices thick-cut Italian bread

2–4 tablespoons melted sweet butter, for grilling

2 tablespoons fresh chopped basil

2 slices provolone cheese

2 slices whole-milk mozzarella cheese

❶ To make the meatballs, combine the first 7 ingredients in a large bowl. Slowly add the milk, mixing with your hands or a fork, until the mixture is slightly moist and can hold its shape. Form the mixture into approximately a dozen 1" meatballs.

❷ Heat oil over medium heat in a large skillet. Fry meatballs in batches so that you have room to maneuver them, turning once the meatballs no longer stick to the pan. After each batch browns on all sides, remove it to a plate. When all of the meatballs are brown all over, pour out the fat that has accumulated in the pan, and then place the entire batch of meatballs back into the pan. Add the marinara sauce, let simmer for 5 minutes, and then remove from heat while you prepare the rest of the sandwich.

❸ Brush the melted butter on the outside of the 2 slices of bread. In a sauté pan, place 1 slice of bread butter side down.

❹ Place the basil, slices of cheese, and 2 or 3 meatballs with approximately 2 tablespoons of sauce on the bread in the pan. Place other slice of bread on top, butter side up. If you are having difficulty closing the sandwich, slice the meatballs in half for a better fit.

❺ Let sandwich cook on medium heat for 3–5 minutes per side or until bread is golden brown. Cut on the diagonal and serve warm.

Fusion Salmon Piccata

Serves 1

1 piece of salmon filet, ⅓ pound, skin removed

Salt and pepper to taste

2–4 tablespoons melted sweet butter, for grilling

2 slices challah bread, hand-cut

2 slices marble cheese

Lemon zest to cover salmon

½ tablespoon guacamole

½ tablespoon capers

Packed with omega-3 fatty acids, protein, and vitamins, salmon is hot for those who are looking for a healthy food. But just because something is healthy doesn't mean it has to be boring! This sandwich celebrates salmon in a uniquely cheesy—and unbelievably delicious—way.

❶ Preheat oven to 375°F. Season salmon with salt and pepper to taste. Bake for 12 minutes. Remove from oven.

❷ Brush the melted butter on the outside of the 2 slices of bread. In an unheated sauté pan, place 1 slice of bread butter side down. Place 1 slice of marble cheese on top of bread followed by the cooked piece of salmon. Spread the lemon zest on top of the salmon, followed by the guacamole, capers, and final piece of cheese. Place other slice of bread on top, butter side up. Turn burner to medium heat.

❸ Let sandwich cook for 5 minutes per side or until bread is golden brown.

❹ Cut on the diagonal and serve hot.

Tips from the Stovetop

The ingredients found in marble cheese depend on the variety of cheese you buy. Some types are simply a combination of white and orange cheddar, while others are a combination of white and yellow Colby, Colby and Monterey jack, or Cheddar and mozzarella.

Ahi Tuna Steak Melt

1 small ahi tuna steak

Salt and pepper, to taste

1 teaspoon teriyaki sauce

½ tablespoon olive oil

1 rustic sandwich roll, sliced horizontally

2 canned pineapple rings

¼ cup Chihuahua cheese

The typical tuna melt with albacore tuna has been done a million times in school lunchrooms all over the country. The finessed version of this favorite replaces out-of-the-can tuna with fresh ahi tuna to take the taste over the top.

❶ Preheat oven 325°F.

❷ Marinate ahi tuna with salt and pepper to taste and brush on teriyaki sauce. Let sit at room temperature for at least 10 minutes prior to cooking.

❸ Heat olive oil in a sauté pan at medium-high heat. Add ahi tuna and sear for 1 or 2 minutes per side.

❹ On an ungreased baking sheet, construct the sandwich. Place cooked tuna on bottom half of sandwich roll followed by pineapple rings and Chihuahua cheese. Close sandwich with other half of bread.

❺ Bake for 3 minutes to let cheese melt. Remove from oven, cut on the diagonal, and serve hot.

Curried Egg Salad

2 hard-boiled eggs, chopped

⅛ cup Hellmann's mayonnaise

¼ teaspoon fresh lime juice

1 teaspoon green onion, sliced

½ tablespoon celery, chopped

1 tablespoon Dijon mustard

⅛ teaspoon curry powder

Pinch of cayenne

½ cup shredded Asiago cheese, divided

2–4 tablespoons melted sweet butter, for grilling

2 slices honey whole wheat bread

When you think of things to add to a grilled cheese sandwich, traditional egg salad may not be one of them. But add some curry, cayenne, Dijon mustard, and Asiago cheese and you end up with a spicy hot grilled cheese that will blow your mind.

❶ In a bowl, thoroughly mix hard-boiled eggs, mayonnaise, lime juice, green onion, celery, Dijon, curry powder, and cayenne. Add in ¼ cup of shredded Asiago and combine.

❷ Brush the melted butter on the outside of the 2 slices of bread. In an unheated sauté pan, place 1 slice of bread butter side down. Place egg salad and the other ¼ cup of shredded Asiago cheese on the bread. Top off the sandwich with the other slice of bread, butter side up. Turn burner to medium heat.

❸ Let sandwich cook for 3–5 minutes per side or until bread is golden brown.

❹ Cut on the diagonal and serve warm.

Tips from the Stovetop

Depending on your love of spice and heat, increase or decrease the amount of curry or cayenne in the egg salad. If you are feeling daring, add an additional ⅛ teaspoon of curry and, instead of a pinch of cayenne, use ⅛ teaspoon.

The Updated Caprese

2–4 tablespoons melted sweet butter, for grilling

2 slices rosemary bread

1 tablespoon store-bought basil pesto

2–3 slices heirloom tomatoes

4 ciliegine fresh mozzarella balls, halved

An insalata caprese salad typically consists of sliced tomato, fresh basil, and fresh buffalo mozzarella—and it is delicious! This recipe takes the delicious and turns it into something unbelievably decadent and gourmet with just a little basil pesto, fresh mozzarella, and sliced heirloom tomatoes all grilled together on fresh rosemary bread.

❶ Brush the meted butter on the outside of the 2 slices of bread. In an unheated sauté pan, place 1 slice of bread butter side down. Spread the basil pesto on the bread, followed by the heirloom tomatoes and fresh mozzarella. Place other slice of bread on top, butter side up. Turn burner to medium heat.

❷ Let sandwich cook for 3–5 minutes per side or until bread is golden brown.

❸ Cut on the diagonal and serve warm.

Soup-less French Onion

Serves 1

1 tablespoon + 1 teaspoon sweet
  butter

½ medium white onion, sliced into
  rings

1 tablespoon white wine

2 cloves garlic, chopped

2–4 tablespoons melted sweet
  butter, for grilling

2 slices sourdough bread

1½ teaspoons dried onion
  soup mix

½ cup shredded Gruyère cheese

Rothbury Farms Buttery Garlic
  croutons, to taste

Everyone loves the cheesy warmth found in French Onion soup, but that perennial favorite isn't all that convenient if you're on the go. Fortunately, with this Soup-less French Onion grilled cheese you can have your soup—and eat it, too.

❶ In a sauté pan, melt 1 tablespoon plus 1 teaspoon sweet butter. Add onion and white wine and sauté on medium heat until onions begin to caramelize, about 10 minutes. Approximately halfway through the caramelization process, add the chopped garlic. Stir occasionally. After cooking, remove onions and garlic from pan and set aside. Do not clean pan.

❷ Brush the melted butter on the outside of the 2 slices of bread. In the same sauté pan place 1 slice of bread butter side down. Place caramelized onions on the bread, followed by the onion soup mix and shredded Gruyère cheese. Crush garlic croutons, to taste, on top of cheese. Place other slice of bread on top, butter side up. Turn burner to medium heat.

❸ Let sandwich cook for 3–5 minutes per side or until bread is golden brown.

❹ Cut on the diagonal and serve warm.

The Mediterranean

Approximately 1 tablespoon olive oil, for baking

½ pita shell

1 cup marinated Mediterranean vegetables

⅓ cup feta

The inclusion of pre-marinated Mediterranean vegetables makes this stuffed pita grilled cheese a perfect sandwich for someone in a hurry. Check your local grocery stores and farmers' markets for olive bars, where you will most likely find a great mix of marinated Mediterranean vegetables that would be perfect for this sandwich.

❶ Preheat oven to 375°F.

❷ Spread olive oil around the outside of the entire pita.

❸ Toss marinated vegetables with feta and stuff inside the pita.

❹ Place on baking sheet and bake for approximately 5 minutes. Serve whole and warm.

Prosciutto and Arugula

2–4 tablespoons melted sweet butter, for grilling

2 slices thick-cut focaccia bread

¼ cup Parmesan cheese, very finely grated

1 slice whole-milk mozzarella cheese

5–6 slices thin cut Prosciutto di Parma

½ cup arugula leaves

2 tablespoons diced pepperoncini peppers

½ cup cherry tomatoes, sliced in half

This upscale guest recipe combines the vibrant flavors of an Italian antipasto with the down-home deliciousness of a great grilled cheese. Parmesan cheese is difficult to melt properly, so you'll need to very finely grate real Parmesan, and layer it with a meltier cheese, such as the mozzarella used here.

❶ Brush the melted butter on the outside of the 2 slices of focaccia bread. In an unheated sauté pan, place 1 slice of bread butter side down.

❷ Layer the focaccia with the rest of the sandwich ingredients, placing the cheeses on the bread first. Turn burner to medium heat.

❸ Let sandwich cook for 3–5 minutes per side or until bread is golden brown.

❹ Cut on the diagonal and serve warm.

Roasted Brussels Sprouts with Cheddar

Serves 1

6 medium/large Brussels sprouts

2 cloves fresh garlic

1 tablespoon chopped green onion

½ tablespoon balsamic vinegar

¾ cup shredded sharp white Cheddar

2½ tablespoons slivered almonds

½ pita shell

Olive oil

Brussels sprouts seem to have a stigma attached to them, but after you try this sandwich, you will stop going out of your way to avoid them. Packed full of almonds, balsamic vinegar, and fresh garlic, one bite of this unreal grilled cheese will banish every negative thought you ever had about these misunderstood veggies. So give Brussels sprouts a shot . . . you may be surprised by how much you like them after all.

1. Preheat oven to 375°F.
2. In a baking pan, combine the Brussels sprouts, garlic, chopped green onion, and balsamic vinegar. Bake for 5 minutes.
3. Once the Brussels sprout mixture is cooked, remove it from oven (do not turn oven off). Place mixture in a bowl and mix in sharp white Cheddar cheese and slivered almonds.
4. Brush outside of pita with olive oil and stuff with Brussels sprouts mixture. Place stuffed pita on baking sheet.
5. Bake in oven just long enough until cheese is melted and pita begins to turn crispy (about 5 minutes). Serve whole and warm.

Crème Fraîche with Apple and Cucumber

Crème Fraîche with Apple and Cucumber

Serves 1

2–4 tablespoons melted sweet butter, for grilling

2 slices sourdough bread

¼ cup crème fraîche

5 thin slices Golden Delicious apple, peeled leaving a minimal amount of skin

6 medium slices salad cucumber, peeled leaving a minimal amount of skin

If you're looking for a sandwich that won't weigh you down, you're in the right place. This grilled cheese sandwich is extremely light and delicious and leaves you feeling satisfied and content . . . and maybe wanting more.

❶ Brush the melted butter on the outside of the 2 slices of bread. In an unheated sauté pan, place 1 slice of bread butter side down. Spread crème fraîche on bread.

❷ Place the apples, followed by cucumbers, on top of crème fraîche. Place other slice of bread on top, butter side up. Turn burner to medium heat.

❸ Let sandwich cook for 3–5 minutes per side or until bread is golden brown.

❹ Let sandwich sit for 3 minutes. Cut on the diagonal and serve warm.

Tips from the Stovetop

It is important to note that the crème fraîche will run a bit upon cooking, so if yours looks a little runny it's nothing to worry about. Allowing the sandwich to sit after cooking will give the crème fraîche time to solidify.

The Blue Potato

FOR POTATOES

2 roasted red potatoes, diced

¼ teaspoon vegetable oil

⅛ teaspoon onion powder

⅛ teaspoon dried dill

⅛ teaspoon paprika

FOR MIXTURE

¼ cup crumbled blue cheese

1½ tablespoons Hellmann's mayonnaise

¼ teaspoon lemon zest

FOR "BREAD"

2 iceberg lettuce leaves

If you think that all grilled cheese sandwiches come squished between two pieces of bread, think again! This unique sandwich walks over the line and uses iceberg lettuce leaves to hold in all that deliciousness, which creates a new experience that everyone can enjoy.

1 Preheat oven to 350°F.

2 In a bowl combine roasted red potatoes, vegetable oil, onion powder, dried dill, and paprika. Mix thoroughly. On a baking sheet, bake seasoned potatoes for 10 minutes.

3 In a separate bowl, combine crumbled blue cheese, mayonnaise, and lemon zest. Mix thoroughly.

4 Once potatoes are out of the oven and still warm, mix them with blue cheese mixture.

5 Place 1 lettuce leaf on a plate, scoop potatoes on top, and then cover with other lettuce leaf. Enjoy hot!

Tips from the Stovetop

Since this sandwich contains no bread or any gluten, it's perfect for anyone living a gluten-free lifestyle. As always though, when cooking, make sure not to cross-contaminate the ingredients for this sandwich with any gluten ingredients or cooking utensils.

Quinoa Black Bean

Serves 1

¾ cup water

¼ cup quinoa, uncooked

¼ cup canned black beans, rinsed and drained

¼ cup tomatoes, diced

½ tablespoon dried cilantro

½ cup shredded sharp white Cheddar, divided

Salt and pepper, to taste

2–4 tablespoons melted sweet butter, for grilling

2 slices sourdough bread

Today it seems like everywhere you go—from supermarket to farmers' market—you can find healthy quinoa front and center. And when you take into account this grain-like seed's fluffy, creamy, slightly crunchy texture, it's really no surprise! Quinoa is an up-and-coming staple in many people's diets, and the somewhat nutty flavor that comes out when this seed is cooked pairs perfectly with the black beans found in this super-healthy grilled cheese sandwich.

1. Boil ¾ cup water and reduce to a simmer. Add quinoa and simmer, uncovered, for 15 minutes, periodically stirring. Let sit uncovered for 5 minutes.
2. Toss cooked quinoa with black beans, tomatoes, cilantro, and ¼ cup white Cheddar. Season with salt and pepper.
3. Brush the melted butter on the outside of the 2 slices of sourdough bread. In an unheated sauté pan, place 1 slice of bread butter side down. Place quinoa mixture on bread followed by ¼ cup white Cheddar. Place other slice of bread on top, butter side up. Turn burner to medium heat.
4. Let sandwich cook for 3–5 minutes per side or until bread is golden brown.
5. Cut on the diagonal and serve warm.

The Sunday Brunch

Serves 1

2 slices red onion rings

1 bagel, any type, sliced

½ hard-boiled egg, slices

½ cup shredded smoked Gouda

½ to 1 red chili pepper, roasted, stem cut, sliced horizontally

Let's be honest: There are way too many options for Sunday brunch. Do you want breakfast? Do you want lunch? The amazing bagel used in place of bread in this recipe really bridges the gap and gives you the best of both worlds. After all, it's easy to choose what you want when you have a recipe that offers you everything you're looking for. Give it a try. You won't be disappointed.

1. Preheat oven to 375°F.
2. On a baking sheet, build the bagel by placing the red onion rings on the bottom half of the bagel followed by hard-boiled egg slices, smoked Gouda, and roasted red chili pepper.
3. Top with other half of bagel and bake for 5 minutes.
4. Cut in half and serve warm.

Tips from the Stovetop

If you have never hard-boiled an egg before, it is really simple. Place an egg in a saucepan, covered by at least an inch of water. Bring the water to a boil, take the pan off the heat, and then let the egg sit in the water for 12 minutes. Peel the egg and you have a hard-boiled egg! To roast the red chili pepper, simply brush on olive oil and bake at 375°F for 15–20 minutes or until sear marks appear.

Sunflower Gouda Griller

 Serves 1

2–4 tablespoons melted sweet butter, for grilling

2 slices sunflower bread

4–5 marinated artichoke heart pieces

½ cup shredded smoked Gouda

1½ tablespoons sunflower seeds, salted

Sure, sunflower seeds may be the perfect snack for a ballgame, but these healthy treats also pack a big gourmet punch when added to this grilled cheese sandwich. The salty seeds complement the softer artichoke hearts and create a sandwich that is as at home at a picnic with friends as it is at an upscale dinner with guests to impress.

❶ Brush the melted butter on the outside of the 2 slices of sunflower bread. In an unheated sauté pan, place 1 slice of bread butter side down. Place marinated artichoke heart pieces on the slice of bread followed by the shredded smoked Gouda and sunflower seeds. Place other slice of bread on top, butter side up. Turn burner to medium heat.

❷ Let sandwich cook for 3–5 minutes per side or until bread is golden brown.

❸ Cut on the diagonal and serve warm.

White Wine and Mushrooms

Serves 1

1¼ cups assorted mushrooms, quartered (see Tips from the Stovetop)

⅛ cup white wine

3 cloves garlic

1 teaspoon thyme

1 teaspoon chives

2 slices Italian bread

2–4 tablespoons melted sweet butter, for grilling

¼ cup crumbled Raclette cheese

Prior to melting, Raclette cheese has a strong odor. Don't be grossed out. Once it melts, the odor cooks off and all that is left is a creamy, delicious cheese that works perfectly for this particular mushroom mixture.

❶ Heat a nonstick sauté pan to medium heat. Combine mushrooms, white wine, garlic, thyme, and chives. Cook mixture until wine has reduced by approximately half.

❷ Brush the melted butter on the outside of the two slices of bread. In a separate, unheated sauté pan, place 1 slice of bread butter side down. Place mushroom mixture and Raclette cheese on top of bread. Place other slice of bread on top, butter side up. Turn burner to medium heat.

❸ Let sandwich cook for 3–5 minutes per side or until bread is golden brown.

❹ Cut on the diagonal and serve warm.

Tips from the Stovetop

Use any combination of mushroom varieties that you prefer, including baby portobellos, crimini, shiitake, and button. Make sure to wash mushrooms with a dry, soft bristled mushroom brush or wipe with dry paper towel. Do not soak or run under water as mushrooms will become waterlogged.

BBQ Chickpeas

1½ tablespoons barbecue sauce

1 large ciabatta roll, sliced horizontally

3 slices garlic Cheddar cheese

¼ cup chickpeas

½ kosher dill pickle, quartered

1½ tablespoons chopped celery

½ tablespoon chives

For many, the taste of barbecue sauce is tied to weekend cookouts and time spent with friends and family. But barbecue sauce isn't just for a backyard get together anymore. In this recipe, the tangy sauce adds the perfect kick to a gourmet grilled cheese overloaded with chickpeas and kosher dill pickles.

❶ Preheat oven to 350°F.

❷ Spread barbecue sauce on the bottom half of the ciabatta roll. Place roll on a baking sheet.

❸ Place 1½ slices of garlic Cheddar cheese on top of the barbecue sauce, followed by the chickpeas, pickle, chives, and celery. Top with the other 1½ slices of garlic Cheddar cheese and half of ciabatta roll.

❹ Bake for 5 minutes.

❺ Cut on the diagonal and serve warm.

Roasted Garlic Tomato Aioli

This is a simple sandwich with a powerful roasted garlic flavor that is unmatched. This is a simple sandwich with a powerful roasted garlic flavor that is unmatched. To make roasted garlic, simply place garlic in a baking pan, cover with olive oil, and bake in an oven preheated to 350°F for 15–20 minutes. The smell will begin to emanate throughout the kitchen when the garlic is ready.

FOR SPREAD

5 cloves roasted garlic, minced

¼ cup Hellmann's mayonnaise

¼ cup tomatoes, medium dice

1 teaspoon olive oil

FOR SANDWICH

2 tablespoons balsamic vinegar, divided

1 small, whole portobello mushroom, sliced into strips

3 ¼" round slices of peeled eggplant

3 ¼" round slices of peeled zucchini

⅛ cup red onion, medium dice

Salt and pepper to taste

2–4 tablespoons melted sweet butter, for grilling

2 slices Italian bread

½ cup shredded sharp white Cheddar cheese

1. In a blender, mix garlic, mayonnaise, tomatoes, and olive oil. Keep tomatoes chunky. Set aside.
2. In a grill pan heated to medium heat, spread 1 tablespoon of balsamic vinegar. Place mushroom, eggplant, zucchini, and onion in pan. Evenly spread the remaining 1 tablespoon of balsamic vinegar on top. Season with salt and pepper. Cook until tender, approximately 10 minutes, flipping once.
3. Brush the melted butter on the outside of the 2 slices of Italian bread.
4. In a separate, unheated sauté pan, place 1 slice of bread butter side down. Spread mayonnaise blend evenly on bread. Stack vegetables on mayonnaise and then top with white Cheddar. Place other slice of bread on top, butter side up. Turn burner to medium heat.
5. Let sandwich cook for 3–5 minutes per side or until bread is golden brown.
6. Cut on the diagonal and serve warm.

Ciliegine with Lime Vinaigrette

Ciliegine with Lime Vinaigrette

The tangy taste of the lime vinaigrette in this recipe makes this sweet, fruity sandwich perfect for either dinner or dessert. Depending on how much lime vinaigrette you use for the sandwich, there may be some left over. Use the extra for fish or even to flavor pasta. Be creative and enjoy.

FOR LIME VINAIGRETTE

⅛ cup dried cilantro

⅛ cup + 1 teaspoon olive oil

⅛ cup lime juice

½ tablespoon orange juice

2 fresh mint stalks, chopped

Salt and pepper, to taste

FOR SANDWICH

2–4 tablespoons melted sweet butter, for grilling

2 slices rosemary bread

2½ fresh ciliegine fresh mozzarella balls, halved

3–5 slices mango (enough to cover mozzarella)

¼ teaspoon dried sweet basil

1. In a bowl, hand-mix cilantro, olive oil, lime juice, orange juice, mint, and salt and pepper. Set vinaigrette aside.
2. Brush the melted butter on the outside of the 2 slices of bread. In an unheated sauté pan, place 1 slice of bread butter side down, followed by the fresh mozzarella and mango. Sprinkle basil and most of lime vinaigrette, to taste. Place other slice of bread on top, butter side up. Turn burner to medium heat.
3. Let sandwich cook for 3–5 minutes per side or until bread is golden brown. Drizzle remaining lime vinaigrette on top of sandwich.
4. Cut on the diagonal and serve warm.

The Spicy Soy

Serves 1

⅓ cup bean sprouts

5 ears of baby corn, chopped

2 tablespoons soy sauce

¼ teaspoon olive oil

2–4 tablespoons melted sweet
   butter, for grilling

2 slices multigrain bread

2 slices hot pepper cheese

¼ cup LaChoy rice noodles

Let's get real: Pretty much everyone loves Chinese food! But who knows what you're really getting in those enticing little boxes? Fortunately, with the combination of soy sauce, rice noodles, and bean sprouts in this recipe, this grilled cheese sandwich will satisfy your Oriental cravings—no MSG included!

❶ In a sauté pan on medium heat, sauté bean sprouts and baby corn in soy sauce and olive oil for 5 minutes or until soy sauce is evenly distributed. Set vegetables aside but do not clean pan.

❷ Brush the melted butter on the outside of the 2 slices of bread. In the same sauté pan, place 1 slice of bread butter side down, followed by 1 slice of hot pepper cheese, the vegetables, the rice noodles, and the other slice of hot pepper cheese. Place other slice of bread on top, butter side up.

❸ Let sandwich cook on medium heat for 5–7 minutes per side or until bread is golden brown.

❹ Cut on the diagonal and serve warm.

Tillamook Cheddar and Baby Bok Choy

½ baby bok choy (stem and leaves)

1 tablespoon sweet butter, for sautéing

Salt and pepper, to taste

2–4 tablespoons melted sweet butter, for grilling

2 slices Tuscan white bread

½ cup shredded mild Tillamook Cheddar

FOR MUSTARD SPREAD

¼ cup Hellmann's mayonnaise

1 tablespoon spicy mustard

2 cloves fresh garlic, chopped

1 teaspoon fresh lemon juice

If you're looking for a smooth sandwich that bites back, this recipe was made for you! The crunch of the bread and bok choy, when experienced in conjunction with the creaminess of the aioli, creates a great contrast in textures that makes this savory sandwich utterly irresistible.

1. Slice stem portion of baby bok choy into strips and set aside. Tear leaves by hand and sauté in 1 tablespoon of butter and salt and pepper, to taste. Cook on medium heat until leaves are wilted. Set aside.
2. In a mixing bowl, thoroughly combine mayonnaise, spicy mustard, garlic, and lemon juice to create mustard spread.
3. Brush 2–4 tablespoons melted butter on the outside of the 2 slices of bread. In an unheated sauté pan, place 1 slice of bread butter side down. Placed wilted baby bok choy leaves on bread, followed by Cheddar cheese, bok choy stems, and mustard spread. Place other slice of bread on top, butter side up. Turn burner to medium heat.
4. Let sandwich cook for 3–5 minutes per side or until bread is golden brown.
5. Cut on the diagonal and serve warm.

Cayenne Cornbread

¼ cup panko bread crumbs

Garlic powder, to taste

Cayenne powder, to taste

1 kumato tomato, sliced (4–5 slices)

Cracked pepper, to taste

2 tablespoons vegetable oil

1 store-bought piece of cornbread, sliced horizontally

⅝ cup shredded Manchego cheese, divided

¼–⅓ cup corn salsa, depending on size of bread

This recipe makes use of the kumato tomato, which is a sweeter tomato that ranges in color from dark brown to golden green. The kumato tomato adds a nice contrast to the savory cornbread. If you are unable to find kumato tomatoes, substitute your favorite variety of tomato.

1. Preheat oven to 375°F.
2. Combine panko bread crumbs, garlic powder, and cayenne powder. Cover tomato slices with the seasoned bread crumbs. Season with cracked pepper.
3. Place oil in a sauté pan. Fry the tomatoes on medium-high heat, flipping once, for approximately 5 minutes or until brown. Remove from heat.
4. Build the sandwich on a baking sheet. On the bottom half of the cornbread place ⅛ cup Manchego, followed by the fried tomatoes, corn salsa, and ¼ cup of Manchego cheese. Place ¼ cup of Manchego cheese on the other half of the cornbread. Do not close the sandwich. Bake for 5 minutes.
5. Close sandwich and serve warm.

Tips from the Stovetop
If you are lucky enough to have a Whole Foods Market in your neighborhood, use their homemade cornbread for this recipe. For an extra kick, try their jalapeño cornbread.

Cayenne Cornbread

The Fried Egg

Serves 1

Most of the ingredients in this grilled cheese are pretty low-key: The egg is soft. The avocado goes down smooth. But don't think that this grilled cheese is boring! Someone invited horseradish to this party, and its unexpected kick enhances the overall flavor and appeal of this feisty sandwich.

1 tablespoon sweet butter, for sautéing

1 jumbo egg

Pepper to taste

2–4 tablespoons melted sweet butter, for grilling

2 slices challah bread, hand-cut

½ cup shredded horseradish white Cheddar cheese

4–5 slices fresh avocado

1 In a sauté pan, heat 1 tablespoon sweet butter until bubbling. Crack egg into pan and season with pepper to taste. Once the egg white has turned solid, flip, and let cook for 2 minutes. Set aside.

2 Brush the melted butter on the outside of the 2 slices of challah bread. In a new sauté pan, place 1 slice of bread butter side down. Place the horseradish cheese on bread, followed by fried egg and avocado slices. Place other slice of bread on top, butter side up. Turn burner to medium heat.

3 Let sandwich cook for 3–5 minutes per side or until bread is golden brown.

4 Cut on the diagonal and serve warm.

The Bacon Filet

1 (4–6-ounce) portion filet mignon

1 teaspoon salt

¼ teaspoon pepper

3–4 slices bacon

2–4 tablespoons melted sweet butter, for grilling

2 slices thick-cut sourdough bread

1 teaspoon whole-grain brown mustard

3 tablespoons crumbled blue cheese

This guest recipe is over-the-top decadent! It takes that old steakhouse favorite, the bacon-wrapped filet, and transforms it into a portable meal! This recipe takes a bit of cooking time and advance prep work to cook the filet, but it's certainly worth it in the end.

❶ An hour before you want to serve the sandwich, remove the filet from the refrigerator. Trim the filet into a uniform cylinder shape, and sprinkle it with the salt and pepper, letting it come to room temperature for 40 minutes or so.

❷ While the filet is resting, preheat a sauté pan over medium heat, and cook the bacon, turning until crisp and brown.

❸ Remove the bacon from the pan and set aside. Pour out all but 3 tablespoons of bacon fat from the sauté pan.

❹ Add the filet to the hot pan and cook, flipping once, until medium-rare (or to your liking), approximately 6 minutes, depending on size of the filet. Remove the filet from the heat, and cut it into thin strips, approximately 1-inch wide.

❺ Heat a separate sauté pan to medium. Brush the melted butter on the outside of the 2 slices of sourdough bread, and brush the insides of the bread with a thin layer of mustard. Place 1 slice of bread in the pan, buttered side down.

❻ On the slice of bread in the pan, layer the mustard, the bacon, the sliced filet, and then the cheese, topping the entire sandwich with the other slice of bread. Turn burner to medium heat.

❼ Let sandwich cook for 3–5 minutes per side or until bread is golden brown.

❽ Cut on the diagonal and serve warm.

Salmon Croquettes with Dill

Salmon Croquettes with Dill

Tuna salad and tuna melts are ubiquitous sandwiches that people just adore. But the salmon croquettes found in this sophisticated recipe give the plain-old tuna melt a run for its money! This high-class recipe turns on your taste buds with a scrumptious sandwich that you won't want to put down.

FOR SALMON CROQUETTES

2 cans pink salmon, skinless/boneless

Pepper, to taste

½ teaspoon parsley

½ teaspoon dill

⅛ teaspoon celery seed

¼ teaspoon dried chives

3 tablespoons red onion, diced

1 jumbo egg

⅛ cup panko bread crumbs

2 tablespoons sweet butter

FOR LEMON DILL MAYONNAISE

½ cup Hellmann's mayonnaise

1 tablespoon dried dill

1 teaspoon lemon zest

FOR SANDWICH

1 ciabatta roll, cut in half and sliced horizontally

½ cup shredded Havarti dill

1. Preheat oven to 350°F.
2. In a mixing bowl, combine all croquette ingredients except butter. Form two patties.
3. In a sauté pan turned to medium heat, cook salmon patties in sweet butter until brown, flipping when necessary. Remove from heat.
4. In a mixing bowl, combine mayonnaise, dried dill, and lemon zest.
5. To form sandwich, place 1 croquette on each bottom piece of bread to form two sandwiches, followed by lemon dill mayonnaise to taste, Havarti dill, and top piece of bread.
6. Bake sandwiches for 5 minutes.
7. Serve hot with any leftover lemon dill mayonnaise on the side.

Asparagus and Lemon Pepper Vinaigrette

Serves 1

The taste of the lemons and pepper found in this sandwich combine to create a sweet and tangy flavor that brings this grilled cheese's freshness to the forefront. Once this sauce is slathered on the curiously crunchy yet soft-on-the-inside sourdough bread, you'll find a sandwich that just has to be savored.

FOR LEMON PEPPER VINAIGRETTE

1 small onion, sliced

2 teaspoons lemon/pepper seasoning salt

1 tablespoon Dijon mustard

1 tablespoon red wine vinegar

½ teaspoon sugar

⅛ cup olive oil

FOR SANDWICH

5 whole asparagus spears

2–4 tablespoons melted sweet butter, for grilling

2 slices sourdough bread

½ cup shredded Dubliner cheese

❶ "Steam" the asparagus in the microwave by placing them in a microwave-safe bowl with enough water to cover the bottom of the bowl. Cook, covered, on high for 30 seconds.

❷ In a mixing bowl, combine all vinaigrette ingredients.

❸ Grill asparagus spears in a grill pan on medium heat, drizzling vinaigrette over asparagus as they cook and continually turning spears so that all sides are covered by the vinaigrette and cook evenly. Set grilled asparagus spears aside.

❹ Brush the melted butter on the outside of the 2 slices of bread. In the same grill pan, place 1 slice of bread butter side down, followed by Dubliner cheese and asparagus spears. Place other slice of bread on top, butter side up.

❺ Let sandwich cook on medium heat for 3–5 minutes per side or until bread is golden brown.

❻ Cut on the diagonal and serve warm.

Asparagus and Lemon Pepper Vinaigrette

Homemade Salsa

Serves 1

With the earthy taste of alfalfa sprouts and the freshness of homemade salsa, the varied flavors in this recipe will keep you on your toes! Challenge your palate with this deliciously distinctive addition to the grilled cheese.

FOR SALSA

2 tomatoes, chopped

1 small tomatillo, chopped

¼ cup fresh cilantro, chopped

1 green onion, chopped

Jalapeño peppers to taste

¼ bell pepper, finely chopped

¼ lime, juiced

Salt, to taste

FOR SANDWICH

2–4 tablespoons melted sweet butter, for grilling

2 slices rye bread

6–7 fresh ciliegine fresh mozzarella balls, halved

¼ cup alfalfa sprouts

❶ In a mixing bowl, combine salsa ingredients.

❷ Brush the melted butter on the outside of the 2 slices of bread. In an unheated sauté pan, place 1 slice of bread butter side down. Place mozzarella halves on the bread, followed by the homemade salsa and alfalfa sprouts. Place other slice of bread on top, butter side up. Turn burner to medium heat.

❸ Let sandwich cook for 3–5 minutes per side or until bread is golden brown.

❹ Cut on the diagonal and serve warm.

Chapter 2

Living on the Edge

When you're talking about savory grilled cheese sandwiches, variety is the spice of life—and the sky's the limit in terms of ingredients when you're living on the edge! Here you'll find that the old standby has been pumped up and allowed to evolve into extraordinary creations. Traditional ingredients such as tomatoes have been replaced with salmon and pasta. Plain mayonnaise is no longer simply spread on bread; it's now mixed with roasted garlic or horseradish to add additional, awesome flavor. And speaking of bread, sometimes it's not even needed! In this chapter, pretzel rolls, potato pancakes, waffles, and even lettuce leaves kick bread to the curb and reign supreme. So buckle your seatbelts! It's going to be a wild ride!

The Deconstructed

Serves 1

2–4 tablespoons melted sweet butter, for grilling

2 small slices challah bread, hand-cut

⅛ cup shredded pepper jack cheese

⅛ cup white onion, diced and caramelized (see Basil Peppercorn recipe in Chapter 1 to learn how to caramelize)

2 slices fresh tomato

2 small slices sharp Cheddar cheese, enough to cover bread

So many options so little time! This deconstructed grilled cheese will have your friends or family loading up their sandwiches and then coming back for more! Here, guests make their own sandwich from ingredients arrayed on a platter, just waiting to be consumed. What you want is what you get! And there's nothing wrong with that!

1 Turn burner to medium heat. Brush melted butter on the outside of the 2 slices of bread. Cook bread in a sauté pan for 3–5 minutes per side or until bread is golden brown. Set aside.

2 In the same hot sauté pan, place shredded pepper jack cheese and cook on medium to medium-high heat until cheese coagulates and creates a single continuous piece, also known as a cheese crisp. Set aside.

3 In a long rectangular dish or your favorite platter, set the toasted bread, caramelized onion, tomato slices, cheese crisp, and sliced Cheddar cheese next to each other. Serve deconstructed.

Sweet and Spicy Popcorn

Serves 1

- ½ teaspoon + to taste Kernel Season's Nacho Cheddar popcorn seasoning
- 1 cup of buttered but unflavored microwave popcorn, popped fresh
- 2–4 tablespoons melted sweet butter, for grilling
- 1 slice Italian bread
- ½ cup + 1 tablespoon shredded provolone cheese
- Caramel syrup and/or crushed red pepper flakes to taste (optional)

They say that once you pop you can't stop, and that's certainly true for this popcorn-covered grilled cheese sandwich! Be sure to use bagged popcorn that's already been popped, because the seasoning will stick better to the kernels and provide a better flavor overall. And for this sandwich, more is more—so, while cooking this amazing sandwich, don't be afraid to add more popcorn to ensure that you end up with a complete top.

1. Pop popcorn in the microwave as directed on the package. Open the bag and sprinkle in ½ teaspoon popcorn seasoning. Shake bag.
2. Brush the melted butter on the outside of the bread.
3. In an unheated sauté pan, place slice of bread butter side down. Evenly spread ½ cup shredded provolone over bread.
4. On top of cheese, place the seasoned popcorn, creating a top to the sandwich. Sprinkle, to taste, more popcorn seasoning and the remaining 1 tablespoon of shredded provolone cheese. Turn burner to medium heat.
5. Cover sandwich and let cook until cheese is melted and popcorn won't fall off.
6. Drizzle sandwich with caramel sauce and/or red pepper flakes if desired and serve warm.

Veggies and Dip

Serves 1

Whether you're getting ready for the big game or hosting friends and family for dinner, veggies and dip are a must. But just because you're the host doesn't mean that you need to spend the night in the kitchen. Cut down on your dirty dishes by combining all your appetizers into one easy-to-eat sandwich and actually spend time with all those people you invited over.

1½ cups mixed, raw veggies

Dill to taste

1½ tablespoons ranch dressing

2–4 tablespoons melted sweet butter, for grilling

2 slices pumpernickel bread, from round loaf

1½ ounces crumbled fresh goat cheese

1. In a bowl, toss veggies with dill to taste and ranch dressing.
2. Brush the melted butter on the outside of the 2 slices of bread. In an unheated sauté pan, place 1 slice of bread butter side down. Spread goat cheese on bread, sprinkle with more dill to taste, and place veggies on top. Cover with other slice of bread, butter side up. Turn burner to medium heat.
3. Let sandwich cook for 3–5 minutes per side or until bread is golden brown.
4. Cut on the diagonal and serve warm.

Tips from the Stovetop
For the veggies, use any that you prefer with ranch dressing, including all peppers, cherry tomatoes, and/or carrots. Make sure to slice veggies on the thinner side to insure easy construction and closing of grilled cheese sandwich.

The Unusual Reuben

Serves 1

1 piece of fresh tilapia (or your favorite light, white fish)

Salt and pepper, to taste

2–4 tablespoons melted sweet butter, for grilling

2 slices seeded rye bread

4 teaspoons Thousand Island dressing, divided

2 slices Swiss cheese

¼ cup sauerkraut or ¼ cup coleslaw

A traditional Reuben contains corned beef, Swiss cheese, sauerkraut, and Thousand Island dressing, which is fine. But if you're looking for something outside of the box, fine isn't good enough. This recipe takes the Reuben over the edge by replacing the red meat with fish, and the sauerkraut with coleslaw. Interesting and unexpectedly delicious!

1 Preheat oven to 325°F.

2 Season tilapia with salt and pepper to taste. Bake for 8 minutes on a greased baking sheet.

3 Brush the melted butter on the outside of the 2 slices of bread. In an unheated sauté pan, place 1 slice of bread butter side down. Spread 2 teaspoons of Thousand Island dressing on the bread, followed by the cooked piece of tilapia. Place the 2 slices of Swiss cheese on top of fish. Place the remaining 2 teaspoons of Thousand Island on the cheese. Top with the sauerkraut or coleslaw. Place other slice of bread on top, butter side up. Turn burner to medium heat.

4 Let sandwich cook for 5 minutes per side or until bread is golden brown.

5 Cut on the diagonal and serve warm.

Fish 'N Chips

Serves 1

Fish and chips is typically just that: fish and chips. However, no one says that these ingredients can't be pumped up to create a fish 'n chips grilled cheese! Piled on top of each other, the blend of the crispy chips and mild fish meld together with the sharpness of the cheddar. Add on the creaminess of the coleslaw and you have one over-the-top Fish 'N Chips grilled cheese!

FOR BATTER

¾ cup flour

1 egg, beaten

¼ teaspoon salt

Dash of pepper

½ cup of your favorite beer

¼ teaspoon lemon zest

FOR FISH

1 medium piece cod

Salt and pepper, to taste

Vegetable oil, enough to cover bottom pan

1 handful frozen shoestring fries, to cover fish, cooked according to package (optional)

2 tablespoons tartar sauce (plus more to serve as side, if desired)

1 hoagie roll, cut horizontally

⅓ cup sharp white Cheddar cheese

1 tablespoon coleslaw

Vegetable oil, enough to cover bottom pan

❶ Preheat oven to 325°F.

❷ To make the batter, combine all batter ingredients and mix until smooth. Set aside in refrigerator.

❸ Season fish with salt and pepper to taste. Heat oil in sauté or frying pan to medium-high heat. Make sure not to scorch oil. Dredge fish in batter and let extra batter drain. Place fish in frying pan, cooking 2–3 minutes per side. Set fish on paper towel to drain excess oil.

❹ Place tartar sauce on roll, followed by fish, cheese, coleslaw, and fries if desired. Bake in oven for 3 minutes.

❺ Cut and serve warm. Serve with additional tartar sauce if desired.

Fish 'N Chips

Sea Salt Hummus

Serves 1

¼ cup garlic hummus

1 ciabatta, sliced horizontally

½ cup sea salt and vinegar potato chips, lightly crushed

½ cup Chihuahua cheese

⅛ teaspoon garlic or regular olive oil

The texture and taste of hummus, a Mediterranean dish made from mashed chickpeas, pairs perfectly with salty chips or pita. In this grilled cheese recipe, garlic hummus is paired with sea salt and vinegar potato chips, which combines the creamy with the crunchy and the awesome with the amazing!

1. Preheat oven to 350°F.
2. Evenly spread the garlic hummus on both the bottom and top halves of the roll. Place 1 slice of the roll on a baking sheet then place crushed sea salt and vinegar potato chips on top of hummus.
3. Spread Chihuahua cheese over chips. Close sandwich with top half of roll. Brush top of roll with garlic olive oil.
4. Bake sandwich in oven for 8 minutes. Serve whole and warm.

Tips from the Stovetop

As hummus becomes more and more popular, the varieties have become endless. Garlic, caramelized onion, and roasted red pepper are just a few types that you will find in your local grocery. Make your grilled cheese custom-suited for you by experimenting with the many unusual flavors.

Green Tea Tofu

1 green tea bag

¾ cup hot water

Fresh or dried mint, to taste

2–3 ounces plain, semi-firm tofu

2–4 tablespoons melted sweet butter, for grilling

2 slices wheat (or multigrain) bread

½ cup shredded Gruyère cheese

You may not think of tofu as grilled-cheese compatible, but this ingredient is actually pretty perfect if you're looking to pack in the flavor. Tofu attracts the essence of anything that it is seasoned or cooked with, and in this recipe, the tofu absorbs the refreshing flavor of green tea and mint. Make this sandwich your own by throwing some other tea flavors into the mix if you're so inclined.

1. In a tea cup, use the green tea bag and water to brew 1 cup of tea for 10 minutes. Place tofu in the tea cup, making sure to leave the tea bag untouched. After 15 minutes, add mint to taste. Let green tea tofu steep for an additional 30 minutes.

2. Brush the melted butter on the outside of the 2 slices of bread. In an unheated sauté pan, place 1 slice of bread butter side down. Cut the tofu pieces in half and place on bread. Cover tofu with Gruyère cheese. Place other slice of bread on top, butter side up. Turn burner to medium heat.

3. Let sandwich cook for 3–5 minutes per side or until bread is golden brown.

4. Cut on the diagonal and serve warm.

The Ramen

2 cups water

⅓ of 3-ounce package ramen noodles

9 snow peas, ends cut and chopped

3 button mushrooms

1 tablespoon teriyaki sauce

¼ teaspoon olive oil

¼ teaspoon Chinese Five Spice

2–4 tablespoons melted sweet butter, for grilling

2 slices rosemary bread

¼ cut ricotta salata

In Asian cooking it's important to incorporate both the yin and yang into a meal: A crunchy dish should have a smooth ingredient, a hot dish should have a cooling ingredient, and so forth. In this recipe, the mix of ground star anise, Szechuan peppercorns, cinnamon, cloves, and fennel seeds found in Chinese Five Spice provides a great blend of sweet, spicy, warm, and cool in one bottle to keep your grilled cheese in balance. You should be able to find Chinese Five Spice at your local grocery store.

❶ In a saucepan, boil water and bring to a simmer. Add in ramen noodles and simmer until soft, approximately 10 minutes. Drain noodles and set aside.

❷ In a sauté pan, sauté cooked ramen noodles, snow peas, button mushrooms, teriyaki sauce, olive oil, and Chinese Five Spice on medium heat for about 7–10 minutes, mixing regularly. Set noodles and vegetables aside but do not clean sauté pan.

❸ Brush the melted butter on the outside of the 2 slices of bread. In the same sauté pan, place 1 slice of bread butter side down, followed by the noodle/vegetable mixture. Sprinkle with ricotta salata cheese. Place other slice of bread on top, butter side up.

❹ Let sandwich cook on medium heat for 3–5 minutes per side or until bread is golden brown.

❺ Cut on the diagonal and serve warm.

The Beer, Kale, and Crouton Mash-Up

The addition of beer in this sandwich, adds a nice crisp, aromatic flavor that enhances the sweet flavor of the pearl onion and makes the sharp Cheddar more powerful. Use your favorite variety of beer to add your own personal touch.

8 pearl onions, halved

1 stalk, destemmed, hand-torn kale

⅛ cup of your favorite beer

Salt, to taste

2–4 tablespoons melted sweet butter, for grilling

2 slices seeded rye

½ cup shredded sharp white Cheddar cheese

¼ cup Rothbury Farms Buttery Garlic croutons

1. In a sauté pan, combine the pearl onions, kale, and beer for approximately 5–7 minutes or until beer has evaporated. Salt to taste. Place mixture to the side.

2. Brush the melted butter on the outside of the 2 slices of bread.

3. In a separate, unheated sauté pan, place 1 slice of bread butter side down. Place kale mixture on top of slice of bread. Place ½ cup of sharp white Cheddar on top. Crush croutons by hand on top of cheese. Cover with other slice of bread, butter side up. Turn burner to medium heat.

4. Let sandwich cook for 3–5 minutes per side or until bread is golden brown.

5. Cut on the diagonal and serve warm.

Tips from the Stovetop

Rothbury Farms Buttery Garlic croutons enhance any dish with their perfectly seasoned crunch and buttery flavor. These particular croutons should be available at your local grocery store. However, if you are unable to find Rothbury Farms Buttery Garlic croutons in your area, feel free to replace them with one of your favorite crouton brands.

The Wedgie

2–4 tablespoons melted sweet butter, for grilling

2 slices pumpernickel bread, from round loaf

1 small wedge iceberg lettuce

⅛ cup red onion

⅛ cup candied pecans

¼ cup + 1 tablespoon blue cheese crumbles

Blue Cheese dressing, to taste

A wedge salad has become ubiquitous on most restaurant menus and if you can put it on a plate, you can put it into an over-the-top grilled cheese. This recipe ups the interest with candied pecans that add a crunchy texture. And if you're missing the bacon that goes on the traditional salad, feel free to add some here.

❶ Brush the melted butter on the outside of the 2 slices of bread. In an unheated sauté pan, place 1 slice of bread butter side down. Place the iceberg wedge on top of the bread and then pile on the red onion, candied pecans, and blue cheese crumbles. Drizzle the blue cheese dressing on top. Cover with other slice of bread, butter side up. Turn burner to medium heat.

❷ Let sandwich cook for 3–5 minutes per side or until bread is golden brown.

❸ Cut on the diagonal and serve warm.

Risotto

When you hear risotto, you may think high-class or upscale, but risotto isn't as snooty as it seems. In fact, risotto is such a creamy, cheesy dish that adding it to a grilled cheese sandwich is a natural next step. In this recipe the cucumber cuts through the risotto's creaminess, bringing a cool, crisp taste to the party.

½ cup cooked Lundberg brand Creamy Parmesan boxed risotto, follow instructions on box (see Tips from the Stovetop)

⅛ cup Asiago cheese

⅛ cup Parmesan cheese

¼ cup diced cucumber

½ teaspoon dried rosemary

½ teaspoon dried dill

2–4 tablespoons melted sweet butter, for grilling

2 slices sunflower seed bread

1. Combine cooked risotto, cheeses, cucumber, rosemary, and dill in a mixing bowl.
2. Brush the melted butter on the outside of the 2 slices of bread. In an unheated sauté pan, place 1 slice of bread butter side down. Place risotto mixture on the bread. Place other slice of bread on top, butter side up. Turn burner to medium heat.
3. Let sandwich cook for 3–5 minutes per side or until bread is golden brown.
4. Cut on the diagonal and serve warm.

Tips from the Stovetop

Cooking risotto from scratch can be an intense process. Using a box simply takes out some of the headache while still producing a great product. Lundberg brand risotto is available at Whole Foods or can possibly be found in the organic aisle of your local grocery store; or simply use your favorite brand of boxed risotto. Add in the seasoning pouch for a more intense cheesy flavor, or simply use the fresh cheese listed above. Use the leftover risotto as a side dish for your next gourmet meal.

The Double Decker

Serves 1

½ cup white onion

¾ cup button mushrooms, sliced

1 teaspoon olive oil

2–4 tablespoons melted sweet
   butter, for grilling

3 slices sourdough bread

½ cup shredded horseradish
   Cheddar cheese

½ cup shredded Parmesan cheese

Hungry? Then it's time to carbo-load! If you're bringing a hearty appetite to the table, then the three pieces of bread used in this recipe are way better than two. The delectable ingredients on the inside of this cheesy piece of heaven are really just the icing on top of this heavy-duty grilled cheese!

1 In a sauté pan, sauté onion and mushrooms on medium heat with olive oil until onions start turning brown and caramelizing, approximately 5–8 minutes. Separate onions and mushrooms. Set aside. Do not clean sauté pan.

2 Brush the melted butter on the outside of two of the slices of bread, leaving the third slice dry. In the same sauté pan, place 1 slice of bread butter side down, followed by the mushrooms and shredded horseradish Cheddar. Place unbuttered slice of bread on top, followed by the caramelized onions and Parmesan cheese. Place other slice of bread on top, butter side up. Turn burner to medium heat.

3 Let sandwich cook on medium heat for approximately 7 minutes per side or until bread is golden brown. (This sandwich may take a couple of extra minutes as it is a double-decker.)

4 Cut on the diagonal and serve warm.

Broccoli Alfredo

⅛ cup frozen peas

1½ cups broccoli florets with minimal stems

Olive oil

Salt and pepper to taste

¼ cup Alfredo sauce

5 leaves of spinach, de-stemmed (optional)

2 slices Italian bread

⅔ cup shredded Parmesan cheese, divided

2–4 tablespoons melted sweet butter, for grilling

If something is inherently creamy and cheesy, it's a perfect candidate to be turned into a grilled cheese! Enter Broccoli Alfredo. It's good on pasta, but even better between two buttery pieces of Italian bread. If you're looking for an even creamier flavor, use ⅓ cup of Alfredo sauce, and if you're a big fan of peas, feel free to bump up that measurement to ¼ cup.

1. "Steam" the broccoli and peas in the microwave by placing them in a microwave-safe bowl with enough water to cover the bottom of the bowl. Cook, covered, on high for 30 seconds.

2. Brush the bottom of a sauté pan with olive oil. Place the broccoli and peas in a sauté pan on medium heat. Season with salt and pepper. Sauté for approximately 5 minutes, or until vegetables are fork-tender.

3. Add Alfredo sauce and mix.

4. Add spinach if desired.

5. Add ⅓ cup of Parmesan cheese. Mix all ingredients until thoroughly incorporated and melted.

6. Brush the melted butter on the outside of the 2 slices of bread.

7. In a separate, unheated sauté pan, place 1 slice of bread butter side down. Place Alfredo mixture on top of bread. Place other slice of bread on top, butter side up. Turn heat to medium.

8. Let sandwich cook for 3–5 minutes per side or until bread is golden brown.

9. Cut on the diagonal and serve warm.

Stuffed Mushrooms

Stuffed Mushrooms

1 portobello mushroom, scooped

¼ cup red onion

⅓ cup red wine

2 cloves garlic, chopped

1 tablespoon butter

¼ cup provolone cheese

¼ cup blue cheese

1 tablespoon olive oil

2 slices avocado

⅛ cup crushed croutons or panko
bread crumbs

Portobello mushrooms are hearty, earthy vegetables that are a perfect stand-in for bread. To scoop out a portobello mushroom, use a small serrated knife to cut out the inner membrane leaving a smooth, concave surface. When scooping the mushrooms for this recipe, make sure not to scoop too deep into the interior. You need enough mushroom to be able to support the blue cheese mixture you will be placing "inside." Stuff. Eat. Enjoy!

❶ Preheat oven to 350°F.

❷ In a sauté pan on medium heat, sauté red onion, red wine, garlic, and butter until liquid has evaporated and onions have softened.

❸ Toss onion mixture with provolone and blue cheese.

❹ Brush outside of mushroom with olive oil. Place avocado slices on inside of mushroom, followed by onion/cheese mixture. Top off with crushed croutons or panko bread crumbs.

❺ In a baking pan, bake stuffed mushroom for 8 minutes.

❻ Serve warm with fork and knife.

Oh! Rings

4–7 frozen onion rings

2–4 tablespoons melted sweet butter, for grilling

2 slices multigrain bread

½ cup shredded horseradish Cheddar cheese

1 tablespoon cocktail sauce

½ tablespoon chives

Let's be honest: Onion rings are pretty perfect. In this recipe, they make grilled cheese perfect, too! Their salty exterior, combined with the pungent taste of the onion and the spicy taste of the horseradish, makes this sandwich so delicious that you'll be coming back for seconds in no time!

1 Cook frozen onion rings according to package directions.

2 Brush the melted butter on the outside of the 2 slices of multigrain bread. In an unheated sauté pan, place 1 slice of bread butter side down. Place horseradish cheese on top of bread, followed by cooked onion rings, cocktail sauce, and chives. Place other slice of bread on top, butter side up. Turn burner to medium heat.

3 Let sandwich cook for 3–5 minutes per side or until bread is golden brown.

4 Cut on the diagonal and serve warm.

Farfalle Pesto Grilled Cheese

Farfalle Pesto Grilled Cheese

Pesto is traditionally made with basil, but in a twist on a classic, this grilled cheese uses a mushroom pesto to enhance the pasta sandwich. This break from tradition ensures that you'll be serving up a grilled cheese that's truly individualized—and unbelievably delicious.

1 cup water

¼ cup uncooked bow tie pasta (farfalle)

2 tablespoons pine nuts

2 shiitake mushrooms, sliced

2 baby portobello mushrooms, sliced

1 tablespoon dried basil

1 tablespoon olive oil

2–3 cherry tomatoes, quartered

¼ cup feta

2–4 tablespoons melted sweet butter, for grilling

2 slices rosemary bread

❶ In a saucepan, boil 1 cup of water. Add pasta and simmer until fork-tender, approximately 10 minutes. Drain pasta and set aside.

❷ In a blender, combine pine nuts, shitake mushrooms, portobello mushrooms, and dried basil. As you are blending, slowly drizzle in the olive oil. Blend until all ingredients are thoroughly mixed. Set aside.

❸ In a large bowl, mix pasta with mushroom pesto, cherry tomatoes, and feta.

❹ Brush the melted butter on the outside of the 2 slices of bread. In an unheated sauté pan, place 1 slice of bread butter side down. Place pasta mixture on bread and top sandwich with other slice of bread, butter side up. Turn burner to medium heat.

❺ Let sandwich cook for 3–5 minutes per side or until bread is golden brown.

❻ Cut on the diagonal and serve warm.

Stuffed Chips

Serves 1

⅓ cup shredded Monterey jack cheese

⅓ shredded smoked Gouda cheese

¼ cup tomato, large dice

5–7 spinach leaves, hand-torn

1 tablespoon green onion, sliced

⅛ cup red onion, small diced

1 pita shell, cut in sixths

1 tablespoon roasted garlic or regular olive oil

½ cup shredded brick cheese

Cracked sea salt, to taste

Crushed tortilla chips, to taste

While homemade sea salt and garlic pita chips are definitely delicious on their own, they become amazing when cheese and vegetables are added. And, in case you were wondering, the toppings for these Stuffed Chips are most definitely not limited to the ingredients listed here. Try it with your own favorite nacho or pizza toppings, too!

❶ Preheat oven to 350°F.

❷ In a bowl, combine Monterey jack cheese, smoked Gouda, tomatoes, spinach, green onion, and red onion. Set aside.

❸ Place pita slices on a baking sheet. Brush garlic olive oil over pita slices. Stuff pita slices with shredded brick cheese. Add cracked sea salt to taste. Bake for 5 minutes and remove from oven. Leave oven on.

❹ Sprinkle cheese/vegetable mixture on top of chips, and add crushed tortilla chips to taste. Bake for an additional 5 minutes.

❺ Serve warm.

Inside-Out Blue Cheese Pecan

Serves 1

⅓ cup caramelized pecans

⅓ cup crumbled blue cheese

2 slices Tuscany bread

1 tablespoon sweet butter, for grilling

⅔ cup shredded sharp Cheddar

This fantastic sandwich turns the everyday grilled cheese inside out—literally! Where the cheese is normally cooked inside the sandwich, in this case, the cheese is actually on the inside and the outside of the sandwich. This process provides a texture and flavor that is not normally found on a traditionally cooked grilled cheese. Instead of experiencing the bread first, your taste buds delve into the nutty flavor and crunchy texture and then the bread. Experiment with different cheeses and nuts to find your favorites!

1 Using a mortar and pestle, crush the caramelized pecans into a powder. Add crumbled blue cheese and integrate into the pecans.

2 Spread the mixture on the outside of the 2 slices of bread. In a sauté pan melt the sweet butter on medium heat and place 1 slice of bread, crusted side down. Sprinkle the Cheddar on top. Place other slice of bread on top, crusted side up.

3 Let sandwich cook for 3–5 minutes per side or until bread is golden brown and crust has formed.

4 Cut on the diagonal and serve warm.

The Savory Waffle

Waffles and eggs are both popular breakfast dishes, but this grilled cheese takes these morning favorites over the top! Perfect for lunch or even dinner, this savory sandwich goes where no waffle has gone before—and we salute it!

2 waffles, cooked

1 tablespoon sweet butter

1 egg

Pepper, to taste

½ cup shredded horseradish white Cheddar cheese

3 slices avocado

1. Preheat oven to 350°F.
2. In a sauté pan, melt the sweet butter on medium heat. Once pan is warm, crack egg into pan. Season egg with pepper to taste. Once the egg white has turned solid, flip, and let cook for 2 minutes. Set aside.
3. On a baking sheet, place 1 slice of horseradish white Cheddar on 1 waffle, followed by fried egg, avocado, and other slice of horseradish white Cheddar. Top with the other waffle.
4. Bake for 5 minutes and serve warm.

Ultimate Cheesy Fries

Ultimate Cheesy Fries

Serves 1

⅓ large, 12" ciabatta (approximately 4 inches in length)

2 Yukon gold potatoes, sliced like thick-cut French fries

¼ teaspoon dried dill, divided

¼ teaspoon paprika

Sea salt, to taste

1 tablespoon vegetable oil, for frying

⅔ cup shredded Monterey jack

1 tablespoon red onion, diced

Ketchup for side (optional)

Shoestring. Wedge. Sweet potato. The list of different French fries just goes on and on. But this recipe takes the ever-popular cheesy fry and turns it into something mouthwateringly over-the-top. After all, why stop with cheese when you can add bread to the mix?

❶ Slice bread horizontally. Discard top or save for another use.

❷ Preheat oven to 350°F.

❸ In mixing bowl, combine sliced potatoes, ⅛ teaspoon dried dill, ⅛ teaspoon paprika, and sea salt to taste. Toss until fries are completely covered.

❹ In a sauté pan, cook seasoned fries in 1 tablespoon oil, on medium heat, continually tossing/stirring. As fries cook, add ⅛ teaspoon dried dill, ⅛ teaspoon paprika, and sea salt to taste. Cook until fries begin to crisp and brown.

❺ Place the cooked fries on top of the ciabatta, followed by Monterey jack cheese and red onion. Bake on a baking sheet for 5 minutes.

❻ Serve warm with side of ketchup, if desired.

Pretzel Baked Beans

Serves 2

Baked beans are typically relegated to the category of "side dish," but here these hearty beans finally steal the show! Combined with a not-so-typical bread made from pretzel rolls, these suddenly-in-the-spotlight baked beans will delight even the hungriest.

1 cup vegetarian baked beans

2 tablespoons barbecue sauce

¼ teaspoon garlic powder

2 tablespoons brown sugar

⅛ cup mushrooms, chopped

⅛ cup onions, chopped

Pinch of dried dill

2 round pretzel rolls, scooped (see Tips from the Stovetop)

½ cup Jarlsberg cheese

❶ In a mixing bowl, combine vegetarian baked beans with barbecue sauce, garlic powder, brown sugar, mushrooms, onions, and dried dill.

❷ Preheat oven to 350°F. In a saucepan, simmer baked bean mixture on medium-high heat for 5–8 minutes, making sure to constantly stir.

❸ Scoop mixture into scooped pretzel roll on baking sheet and cover with Jarlsberg cheese.

❹ Bake for 5 minutes, or until cheese is fully melted.

❺ Serve hot with spoon.

Tips from the Stovetop

A pretzel roll is exactly that: a roll made out of soft pretzel dough. Scooping a pretzel roll is very different from scooping any other typical type of sliced bread. The goal is to keep the flaps intact while removing enough of the insides. A delicate touch is a must. To scoop a pretzel roll, start in the middle. With a small, sharp, pointed knife, get under the flaps and carefully pull out the "innards."

Pretzel Baked Beans

The Scrambled Spanakopita

The Scrambled Spanakopita

Serves 1–2

2 jumbo eggs

3 tablespoons sweet butter, divided

½ cup feta + 2 teaspoons feta to crumble on top

1 package Stouffers Spinach Soufflé

1 package (4-ounce) crescent rolls

Spanakopita is a traditional Greek dish that consists of chopped spinach, feta cheese, onions, eggs, and seasoning. This particular grilled cheese substitutes scrambled eggs and spinach soufflé to create a creamy and scrumptious grilled cheese that overshadows its more traditional Greek cousin.

1. Cook spinach soufflé according to package. Put aside ½ cup for this recipe; store remainder and use as desired.
2. Preheat oven to 375°F.
3. In a small bowl, beat eggs.
4. In a sauté pan, melt 1 tablespoon of sweet butter on medium heat. Add egg and ¼ cup feta, consistently scrambling with a spatula. Cook until nearly firm and still a bit runny.
5. Add ½ cup of cooked spinach soufflé and ¼ cup feta, continuously mixing. Cook until all ingredients are thoroughly mixed then remove from heat.
6. Spray cookie sheet with nonstick spray. Roll crescent rolls out on cookie sheet, separating to make 2 rectangles. Press perforations together. Melt 2 tablespoons of butter and spread on crescent rolls.
7. Equally distribute egg and spinach mixture onto rectangles. Roll up from small end to small end. Bake for 10–11 minutes or until crispy.
8. Serve hot either whole or cut into multiple pinwheels.

The Pizza Volcano

2 teaspoons olive oil

2 kaiser rolls, scooped

¾ cup marinara sauce

⅓ cup Alfredo sauce

1½ tablespoons fresh basil, chopped

1 garlic clove, minced

¾ cup quattro formagio mix (mozzarella, Asiago, smoked provolone, and Romano), divided

3 spears of asparagus, blanched and cut

½ cup mushrooms, diced

Rothbury Farms Buttery Garlic croutons, crushed, to taste (optional)

Pizza on its own is pretty amazing, but this recipe turns pizza on its head. Just think of all the options for sauces and toppings and cheeses! The asparagus and mushrooms used here are really only the tip of the iceberg when it comes to possible ingredients. Choose your favorite pizza toppings to make this grilled cheese your own!

❶ Preheat oven to 350°F.

❷ Spread olive oil on the outside and inside of the scooped kaiser roll.

❸ In a bowl, mix marinara and Alfredo sauces, fresh basil, garlic, and ¼ cup cheese mixture. Pour into kaiser roll. Top with asparagus, mushrooms, and ½ cup of cheese mixture. Sprinkle with crushed garlic croutons, to taste.

❹ Bake for 7 minutes on a baking sheet. Serve warm.

Boneless Buffalo Wings

Serves 1

- 3–4 frozen buffalo chicken tenders
- 2–4 tablespoons Frank's RedHot sauce (any flavor)
- 2 tablespoons blue cheese
- 2 tablespoons sour cream
- 2 tablespoons shredded Cheddar cheese
- 2–4 tablespoons melted sweet butter, for grilling
- 2 slices thick-cut sourdough bread
- 1 tablespoon thinly sliced green onions
- ¼ cup shredded lettuce

Maybe the only thing better than buffalo chicken wings is buffalo nachos—at least, until now! This guest recipe creates a sandwich that takes the best parts of these amazing appetizers and fuses them into one awesome concoction. You can control the heat in the sandwich by either using less sauce, or more condiments!

1. Prepare the frozen buffalo tenders according to the package directions. Frying is the preferred method to retain crispness. Once the tenders are cooked, toss them with the additional Frank's sauce to taste.
2. In a bowl, stir together the sour cream, blue cheese, and Cheddar cheese. Set aside.
3. Brush the melted butter on the outside of the 2 slices of sourdough bread. In an unheated sauté pan, place 1 slice of bread butter side down.
4. Layer the bread with the blue cheese mixture, the chicken tenders, the green onion, and the shredded lettuce. Turn burner to medium heat.
5. Let sandwich cook for 3–5 minutes per side or until bread is golden brown.
6. Cut on the diagonal and serve hot.

The Hashbrown

This grilled cheese recipe is perfect if you wake up craving a crazy breakfast. Packed with potato, cheese, and some veggies for good measure, The Hashbrown is sure to get you out of your PJs and on your way to a good morning!

2–3 tablespoons vegetable oil, for sautéing

1 small potato, peeled and shredded

½ red pepper, small dice

½ green pepper, small dice

½ onion, small dice

Salt and pepper, to taste

2–4 tablespoons melted sweet butter, for grilling

2 slices whole wheat pugliese bread

½ cup shredded Monterey jack cheese

❶ In a sauté pan, heat oil to medium heat. Add shredded potato, red and green peppers, and onion. Stir continuously. Add salt and pepper, to taste. Cook until potatoes begin to brown. Set aside.

❷ Brush the melted butter on the outside of the 2 slices of bread. In a new, unheated sauté pan, place 1 slice of bread butter side down. Place freshly made hashbrowns on the bread followed by shredded Monterey jack cheese. Place the other slice of bread on top, butter side up. Turn burner to medium heat.

❸ Let sandwich cook on medium heat for 3–5 minutes per side or until bread is golden brown.

❹ Cut on the diagonal and serve warm.

The Hashbrown

Fried Matzoh with Horseradish Mayo

¼ cup Hellmann's mayonnaise

1 tablespoon grated fresh horseradish

4 slices matzoh

3 cups water

2 jumbo eggs

Salt, to taste

3 tablespoons sweet butter

½ cup shredded Cantalet cheese, divided

4–5 slices fresh tomato

Just because this sandwich combines many traditional elements of the Jewish holiday of Passover—horseradish, matzoh, and fried matzoh (scrambled eggs mixed with matzoh)—doesn't mean that this grilled cheese should be saved for a solemn occasion. If you're looking for an off-the-beaten-path sandwich to curb your grilled cheese cravings, you've come to the right place!

1. Preheat oven to 350°F.
2. In a mixing bowl, mix mayonnaise and horseradish. Set aside.
3. Crack two pieces of matzoh into small pieces and place in a new mixing bowl with 3 cups water. Let soak.
4. In a separate bowl, crack eggs and beat. Squeeze soaking matzoh free of water and place in bowl with beaten eggs. Mix and add salt, to taste.
5. In a sauté pan, melt sweet butter over medium to medium-high heat. Add matzoh/egg mixture. Cook as you would scramble eggs, stirring continuously, approximately 5–7 minutes. Remove from heat and set aside.
6. Place 1 slice of matzoh on baking sheet. Spread horseradish mayo on 1 slice, followed by ¼ cup Cantalet cheese, matzoh/egg mixture, sliced tomatoes, and the other ¼ cup Cantalet. Top with other slice of matzoh. Bake for 5 minutes or until cheese is fully melted.
7. Serve whole and warm.

Garlic and Green Onion Mashed Potato

Serves 2

3 medium-sized potatoes, unpeeled

4 cups + 2 tablespoons water

8–10 broccoli stems

7 tablespoons melted sweet butter, divided, for cooking

¼ cup + ⅛ cup green onion, cut

Salt and pepper, to taste

⅔ cup milk

5 cloves roasted garlic (for instructions see recipe in Roasted Garlic Tomato Aioli in Chapter 1)

1 tablespoon dried rosemary

2 tablespoons margarine

4 slices Italian bread

½ cup creamy Havarti

½ cup sharp Cheddar cheese

Mashed potatoes are usually relegated to side dish status, but that's not the case with this recipe. This surprising dish puts the mashed potatoes right into the grilled cheese, creating an unexpected but delicious sandwich.

❶ Cut unpeeled potatoes into large chunks.

❷ Boil 4 cups water, add potatoes, and simmer over low heat until potatoes are fork-tender.

❸ While potatoes are simmering, place broccoli stems in a bowl with 2 tablespoons water, covered, and microwave for about 45 seconds–1 minute on high.

❹ In a sauté pan, combine 3 tablespoons of melted butter, broccoli, and ¼ cup green onion. Sauté over medium heat, adding salt and pepper to taste. Cook until broccoli begins to soften. Set aside. Do not clean sauté pan.

❺ When potatoes are done, drain excess water. Add milk, roasted garlic, ⅛ cup green onion, rosemary, margarine, and salt and pepper to taste. Mash until mixture has an almost creamy texture. Set aside.

❻ Brush 4–6 tablespoons melted butter on the outside of the 4 slices of bread. In the same sauté pan, place 2 slices of bread butter side down. Place freshly made mashed potatoes on the 2 slices of bread, followed by broccoli/green onion mixture, shredded Havarti, and shredded sharp Cheddar cheese. Place the other 2 slices of bread on top, butter side up.

❼ Let sandwich cook on medium heat for 5–7 minutes per side or until bread is golden brown.

❽ Cut on the diagonal and serve warm.

The Potato Pancake

The Potato Pancake

Serves 1

½ sweet apple, such as Golden
  Delicious, sliced

1 tablespoon brown sugar

½ teaspoon white sugar

2 large deli/store-bought potato
  pancakes

¼ cup blue cheese

¼ cup crumbled Fontal cheese

Potato pancakes are simply shredded potatoes fried into crispy, flat patties of total deliciousness. To make sure that this grilled cheese is as fresh as possible, purchase fresh potato pancakes from a nearby deli/grocery store; they will be larger and denser than the potato pancakes from the freezer section of your local grocery store. If you do purchase frozen ones, create multiple mini-sandwiches using the same steps.

❶ Preheat oven to 350°F.

❷ In a baking pan, combine sliced apple with brown and white sugar. Bake for 5–8 minutes or until apples are soft and a syrup-like liquid begins to appear. Keep oven on; set apples aside.

❸ Construct sandwich on a new baking sheet. On bottom half of 1 potato pancake, sprinkle blue cheese, followed by cooked apple mixture, crumbled Fontal cheese, and the other potato pancake.

❹ Bake for 5 minutes and serve warm.

The Spicy Dubliner

¼ cup Hellmann's mayonnaise

½ tablespoon spicy brown mustard

4 tablespoons sauerkraut, divided

2–4 tablespoons melted sweet butter, for grilling

2 slices Tuscany bread

⅓ cup shredded Dubliner with Irish Stout cheese

⅓ cup shredded jalapeño Cheddar cheese

Kerrygold's Dubliner with Irish Stout is worth the hunt. Typically available at your local gourmet grocery stores, this sweet and malty cheese adds another layer to this multi-textured grilled cheese. The combined flavors of this grilled cheese meld together to create an explosion in your mouth.

❶ In a mixing bowl, combine mayonnaise, spicy brown mustard, and 3 tablespoons sauerkraut.

❷ Brush the melted butter on the outside of the 2 slices of bread. In an unheated sauté pan, place 1 slice of bread butter side down. Place Dubliner cheese on bread, followed by mayonnaise spread, 1 tablespoon sauerkraut, and jalapeño Cheddar. Place other slice of bread on top, butter side up. Turn burner to medium heat.

❸ Let sandwich cook for 3–5 minutes per side or until bread is golden brown.

❹ Cut on the diagonal and serve warm.

Mini-Eggplant Sliders

Mini-Eggplant Sliders

Serves 1

½ cup panko bread crumbs

1 jumbo egg

2 slices, ½" thick, eggplant, peeled

1 tablespoon olive oil

⅓ cup ricotta cheese or Parmesan cheese

¼ cup tomato sauce + extra ¼ cup for dipping, if desired

1 teaspoon chopped red onion

1 tablespoon dried basil

Not every grilled cheese sandwich needs bread to be complete and, in this case, bread would only serve to detract from these sliders. Here, all you need are two slices of eggplant and your grilled cheese is off to a delicious start!

1. Preheat oven to 350°F.
2. Mix panko bread crumbs and dried basil in a bowl and place cracked egg in a separate bowl. Individually place slices of eggplant in egg and then in bread crumbs, making sure to cover entire slices.
3. Prepare grill pan by warming olive oil to medium heat. Cook coated eggplant slices for 3–5 minutes per side or until coating is crunchy.
4. In a baking pan, place 1 eggplant slice followed by the ricotta or Parmesan cheese, tomato sauce, and chopped red onion. Top with other eggplant slice.
5. Bake for 5 minutes, enough to warm the ricotta or melt the Parmesan, depending on which cheese you have selected.
6. Serve hot with fork and knife.

Big Game Nachos and Cheese

 Serves 1

¼ pound sharp Cheddar cheese

⅛ pound Dubliner cheese

1½ jalapeño peppers, to taste, small diced

1 uncooked pizza shell

7–9 whole yellow corn round tortilla chips

Why buy unnatural, processed nacho cheese when it is so easy to create your own? Depending on your appreciation of spiciness, feel free to increase the amount of jalapeño peppers in this sandwich—or kick this recipe up a notch by using even hotter peppers, such as a Serrano, cayenne, or habanero. Just keep a glass of milk handy to soothe that fiery mouth!

1 Preheat oven to 375°F.

2 Cut the Cheddar and Dubliner cheese into large chunks and place into a bowl. Microwave cheese on high for 45 seconds to 1 minute, or until cheese is completely melted. Mix in jalapeño pieces, including the seeds. Set in refrigerator to coagulate, at least 15 minutes.

3 Using an oval mold of approximately 6.5" in diameter (length) or simply free form, cut two oval shapes into the pizza shell, creating a top and bottom for your sandwich.

4 Take homemade nacho cheese out of refrigerator and cut into chunks. Place chunks on 1 piece of pizza shell followed by whole tortilla chips and second oval pizza shell. Bake for 5–7 minutes or until cheese is fully melted.

5 Cut in half and serve warm.

Part 2

Surprisingly Sweet Stacks

When most people think of grilled cheese sandwiches, they think savory, not sweet. But the recipes found in this section turn that idea totally on its head! Unexpected and maybe even a bit quirky, sweet grilled cheese sandwiches are taking the culinary world by storm—and they're taking names like Boston Cream Pie, Stuffed French Toast, and The Candy Cane as they go. In Chapter 3 you'll find sandwiches made with upscale ingredients like currant jam, pomegranate, brie, and kiwi that are so sophisticated you'll find yourself holding your pinkie finger up while you eat. And in Chapter 4 you'll find sweet grilled cheeses that combine rhubarb, salted caramel, bacon, and other ingredients so crazy you'll be licking your fingers—and the plate!—when they disappear. So get ready to sweeten the pot with these grilled cheese delights!

Chapter 3

Epicurean Adventures

When the original grilled cheese sandwich was invented hundreds of years ago, no one could have expected the evolution from its humble roots to the sweet sandwiches that you'll find here. The pages that follow offer everything from grilled cheeses with sweet potatoes and marshmallows to delicacies that highlight the inherent sweetness in berries and squash. This chapter features sandwiches that showcase the high-quality ingredients that speak to the gourmet level of today's sweetest grilled cheeses. Try them at the end of an already fantastic meal or be daring and try a sweet grilled cheese as the main course. Whatever you decide, you won't be disappointed.

The Nutella

Serves 2

¼ cup goat cheese, softened

¼ cup Nutella

4 pizzelles

Slivered almonds, to taste,
  if desired

1 tablespoon raspberry preserves

Powdered sugar, for decoration

Nutella, a well-known hazelnut spread, can be enjoyed simply with a spoon, but it's even more delectable when it's mixed with goat cheese and slathered onto a grilled cheese sandwich! You don't even need to cook this sweet sandwich. Simply add pizzelles and raspberry preserves to the mix and dessert is served!

1. On a plate, lay out the four pizzelles, bottom side up.
2. In a bowl, mix softened goat cheese with Nutella. Softly distribute the mixture between two pizzelles, the bottom halves of the sandwich. If desired, sprinkle almonds on top of Nutella.
3. Gently spread the raspberry preserves between the two other pizzelles, the tops of the sandwich. Then place them on top of the Nutella pizzelles, preserve side down, closing the two individual sandwiches.
4. Sprinkle pizzelles with powdered sugar for decoration and flavor, and serve at room temperature.

Harvest Fest

The flavors in this sweet recipe—sweet potato, cinnamon, and apple—harken to fall when the leaves have just changed colors and Thanksgiving is right around the corner. However, this combination will help cool you down even if it is the middle of summer and 85°F outside.

1 small-to-medium sweet potato, unpeeled

½ tablespoon sweet butter, melted

2 teaspoons cinnamon sugar

2 tablespoons melted sweet butter, for grilling

2 slices honey whole wheat bread

3 large marshmallows, halved

3–4 slices sweet/soft apple (e.g., McIntosh)

¼ cup Havarti

¼ cup Gruyère

❶ Microwave sweet potato on high for 4–5 minutes, or until fork-tender. Let cool. Peel off skin and discard. Slice potato into ¼ " rounds. Drizzle ½ tablespoon of sweet butter and sprinkle cinnamon sugar onto potato slices.

❷ Brush the remaining melted butter on the outside of the 2 slices of bread. In an unheated sauté pan, place 1 slice of bread butter side down, followed by the sliced sweet potato, marshmallows, apple slices, Havarti, and Gruyère. Place other slice of bread on top, butter side up. Turn burner to medium heat.

❸ Let sandwich cook for 5–7 minutes per side or until bread is golden brown.

❹ Cut on the diagonal and serve warm.

Tips from the Stovetop

Cinnamon sugar is a combination of ground cinnamon and granulated sugar. This mixture is available at your grocery store in the spice aisle.

Honey Roasted PB & J

Serves 1

2–4 tablespoons melted sweet butter, for grilling

2 slices sourdough bread

2 teaspoons honey roasted peanut butter (or enough to cover bread)

1½–2 slices Monterey jack

⅓ banana, sliced

⅛ cup roasted, salted cashews, hand-cracked

1½ teaspoons currant jam

Since bread was first sliced, school kids have been heading off with peanut butter and jelly sandwiches packed away in their lunch bags. You may be grown up now, but with the addition of honey roasted peanut butter and currant jam, this gourmet grilled cheese sandwich has grown up, too.

❶ Brush the melted butter on the outside of the 2 slices of sourdough bread. In an unheated sauté pan, place 1 slice of bread butter side down. Spread honey roasted peanut butter on bread, followed by 1 slice of Monterey jack cheese, banana slices, and cashews. Spread currant jam on other slice of bread, non-butter side, and place on top, butter side up. Turn burner to medium heat.

❷ Let sandwich cook for 3–5 minutes per side or until bread is golden brown.

❸ Cut on the diagonal and serve warm.

Tips from the Stovetop

Substitute your favorite flavors or kinds of nuts and jams for what's in the recipe to add another unique twist to the traditional peanut butter and jelly sandwich. Be creative!

Squash with Apple Butter

Serves 1

1 spaghetti squash

2 tablespoons melted sweet butter, divided

1 tablespoon brown sugar

⅛ cup apple butter

¼ cup cranberry goat cheese, softened

1 croissant, cut horizontally

This squash and apple butter grilled cheese just screams autumn—and the combination of fall flavors makes for a sweet and tangy treat. Bake and mix both halves of the squash and use the additional portion to create a yummy vegetable side dish.

1. Preheat the oven to 350°F. Cut the squash in half, lengthwise. Scoop out the seeds of 1 half and save other half for another use. Bake the half cut side down on a baking sheet for 40 minutes or until tender. Remove from oven and let sit for 5 minutes. Reduce oven temperature to 325°F.

2. With a fork, rake out the squash membrane. Mix the squash with 1 tablespoon sweet butter and brown sugar. Then add the apple butter and mix.

3. Spread the cranberry goat cheese on the bottom half of the croissant, followed by the squash/apple butter mixture. Close sandwich with top half of croissant.

4. On a clean baking sheet bake the sandwich for 3 minutes. Cut in thirds and serve warm.

Tips from the Stovetop

Cranberry goat cheese is a seasonal cheese that is more readily available during the winter months. Search your local gourmet cheese shop or try to make it on your own. Simply take a 4-ounce package of fresh goat cheese and add in 1 tablespoon of fresh cranberries. Increase the amount of cranberries for a more tart flavor.

Marinated Berries

Fresh and fork-and-knife worthy, this particular grilled cheese sandwich takes seasonal fruit to a whole new level of perfection. Who knew that something sweet could be so refreshing!

FOR MARINATED BERRIES

2 tablespoons sugar

½ teaspoon lemon zest

½ teaspoon lime zest

½ teaspoon vanilla extract

½ cup water

3 medium-sized strawberries

1½ ounces raspberries

1½ ounces blackberries

FOR SANDWICH

2–4 tablespoons melted sweet butter, for grilling

2 slices Italian bread

¾ cup shredded yogurt cheese (Use another mild, creamy cheese such as provolone, if yogurt cheese is unavailable in your area.)

2 tablespoons toasted pine nuts (see Tips from the Stovetop)

❶ In a sauté pan, combine sugar, lemon and lime zests, vanilla, and water, stirring periodically. Cook on medium heat until the liquid takes on a syrupy texture, approximately 10 minutes. Remove from heat and place in a small bowl.

❷ Add berries to marinade in bowl and stir gently, making sure all berries are fully covered. Let sit until ready to make grilled cheese and then drain marinade.

❸ Brush the melted butter on the outside of the 2 slices of bread.

❹ In a separate, unheated sauté pan, place 1 slice of bread butter side down. Place berries on top of bread. Follow with yogurt cheese and toasted pine nuts. Place other slice of bread on top, butter side up. Turn burner to medium heat.

❺ Let sandwich cook for 3–5 minutes per side or until bread is golden brown.

❻ Cut on the diagonal and serve warm.

Tips from the Stovetop

Pine nuts can be expensive, even in small amounts, so feel free to substitute your favorite type of nut. If you do decide to use pine nuts, simply place them in a hot oven for a few minutes until they turn a beautiful golden brown. The final product will be perfectly toasted pine nuts.

Marinated Berries

Coconut Peach

½ cup cottage cheese

5 canned peach slices,
  cut in thirds

1 teaspoon peach juice,
  found in can

3 teaspoons brown sugar, divided

1 croissant, sliced horizontally

1 teaspoon flaked coconut

The combination of cottage cheese and peaches is popping up everywhere from beachside bistros to summertime farm stands. This recipe offers an extra layer of sophistication to this fresh dish by adding brown sugar and placing it into a flaky croissant. If you're not a fan of peaches, substitute with your favorite sweet fruits to guarantee that you're getting what you love!

❶ Preheat oven to 350°F.

❷ In a bowl, combine cottage cheese, sliced peaches, peach juice, and 2 teaspoons brown sugar. Place on croissant. Sprinkle the remaining brown sugar on top, followed by the flaked coconut.

❸ Top with the other half of the croissant and bake for 5 minutes.

❹ Slice in thirds and serve warm.

Kicked-Up Mint

Serves 1

From mojitos to mint chocolate chip ice cream, mint rules supreme! In this grilled cheese, fresh mint is turned into a chutney-like substance that adds great flavor and an upscale kick. Mint is an herb that easily and quickly grows in any garden; maybe this recipe will inspire you to grow your own.

FOR MINT MIXTURE

⅛ cup fresh mint, chopped

1 teaspoon olive oil

½ tablespoon red onion, chopped

⅛ teaspoon dried cilantro

FOR SANDWICH

2–4 tablespoons melted sweet
    butter, for grilling

2 slices honey whole wheat bread

3 slices hot pepper cheese

1½ slices heirloom tomato

2 slices red pepper

2 slices yellow pepper

❶ In a bowl, mix mint, olive oil, red onion, and dried cilantro with a fork. Set aside.

❷ Brush the melted butter on the outside of the 2 slices of bread. In a sauté pan, place 1 slice of bread butter side down. Place 1½ slices of hot pepper cheese on bread, followed by the vegetable slices. Turn burner to medium heat.

❸ Drizzle mint mixture on top, followed by the other 1½ slices of hot pepper cheese. Place other slice of bread on top, butter side up.

❹ Let sandwich cook for 3–5 minutes per side or until bread is golden brown.

❺ Cut on the diagonal and serve warm.

The Tropical

3 tablespoons sweet butter, divided

⅔ whole nectarine, peeled and sliced

¼ whole mango, peeled and sliced

3 teaspoons brown sugar, divided

1 piece plain naan bread, halved

½ cup ricotta cheese

The naan used in this recipe is a traditional Asian flatbread that is perfect when simply brushed with olive oil and baked. Naan does come in multiple flavors, including whole wheat or garlic, but for this sandwich it is definitely recommended to use plain naan, which will allow the sweetness of the fruit to shine.

1. Preheat oven to 350°F.
2. In a grill pan, melt 2 tablespoons of butter. Grill nectarine and mango slices in pan on medium heat for approximately 3–5 minutes per side, or until grill marks have appeared. Prior to turning fruit, sprinkle 2 teaspoons of brown sugar on fruit. Remove from heat and set aside.
3. Spread remaining tablespoon of sweet butter on outside of both halves of naan bread.
4. On bottom slice of naan bread, spread ricotta cheese, followed by remaining teaspoon of brown sugar. Cover with grilled fruit and then close sandwich with the top half of the naan bread.
5. Bake sandwich on a baking sheet for 8 minutes. For a crunchier texture, broil the sandwich on low for 1–2 additional minutes.
6. Sprinkle sandwich with 1 teaspoon brown sugar and serve warm with knife and fork.

Currant Jam

2–4 tablespoons melted sweet
  butter, for grilling

2 slices multigrain bread

2 tablespoons currant preserve

½ cup shredded Jarlsberg cheese

½ cup arugula, de-stemmed

Forget the standard grape jelly that you've been slathering on sandwiches for years, and get ready to try a unique currant preserve instead! Currants—a dried, black, seedless grape—have a sweet, tart taste that pairs well with many dessert foods such as ice cream or a tart.

❶ Brush the melted butter on the outside of the 2 slices of bread. In an unheated sauté pan, place 1 slice of bread butter side down. Spread currant preserve on bread followed by cheese and arugula. Place other slice of bread on top, butter side up. Turn burner to medium heat.

❷ Let sandwich cook for 3–5 minutes per side or until bread is golden brown.

❸ Cut on the diagonal and serve warm.

Walnut Pomegranate

2–4 tablespoons melted sweet butter, for grilling

2 hand-cut slices challah

Brie to coat bread, approximately 4 ounces

3 tablespoons pomegranate seeds

2 tablespoons walnuts

The pomegranate is an intriguing and exotic fruit that makes a wonderful juice. The pomegranate has ancient roots in the Middle and Near East and dates back more than 4,000 years. This fruit provided both nutrition and sustenance during long-distance journeys. The seeds, also known as jewels, add a great crunchy texture to a grilled cheese sandwich, while also providing a tart flavor.

1. Brush the melted butter on the outside of the 2 slices of bread. In a sauté pan, place 1 slice of bread butter side down. Coat bread with brie.
2. Sprinkle pomegranate seeds and walnuts on top of brie. Place other slice of bread on top, butter side up. Turn burner to medium heat.
3. Let sandwich cook for 5 minutes per side or until bread is golden brown.
4. Cut on the diagonal and serve warm.

Tips from the Stovetop

Prior to cutting into a pomegranate, make sure you are using a plastic cutting board and clothes you don't care about as to avoid staining. Working over a bowl helps keep the splashing from staining your clothes. Cut the pomegranate in half, through the stem, or crown. Then cut the halves in half. Using a spoon, or your fingers, dig out the required seeds, or jewels, for this grilled cheese recipe. Munch on the remaining seeds as a healthy snack.

Apple Pie

⅓ large ciabatta, 12" total (4 inches in length)

3 tablespoons sweet butter, divided

1 golden delicious apple, unpeeled and thinly sliced

1 tablespoon + ¾ teaspoon brown sugar, divided

1 tablespoon white sugar

½ teaspoon cinnamon

¼ pound MT TAM cheese by Cowgirl Creamery

Walnuts, to taste (optional)

½ graham cracker, cracked into small to medium-sized pieces

Apple pie is as American as . . . well . . . apple pie. But in this sandwich, it goes gourmet with a distinctive organic cheese from Cowgirl Creamery that works to add a creamy texture and earthy flavor. If you are unable to find MT TAM cheese in your area, replace with either brie or Camembert cheeses.

❶ Slice ciabatta horizontally. Discard top or save for another use.

❷ In a sauté pan on medium heat, cook 2 tablespoons sweet butter, apple slices, 1 tablespoon brown sugar, white sugar, and cinnamon, continually stirring. Cook until apples are limp and mixture has a syrupy consistency, approximately 10 minutes. Do not drain. Set aside.

❸ Preheat oven to 350°F.

❹ Spread 1 tablespoon of sweet butter on bread, followed by ½ teaspoon of brown sugar, MT TAM cheese, cooked apples, and syrup from pan. Crush walnuts on top if desired, followed by cracked graham cracker. Sprinkle ¼ teaspoon of brown sugar on top of sandwich.

❺ Bake sandwich on a baking sheet for 5 minutes.

❻ Remove from oven and serve hot.

Tips from the Stovetop

Apple pie is routinely served "à la mode," or with ice cream. Add a scoop of your favorite ice cream on top of this apple pie grilled cheese for an even more delectable dessert.

Apple Pie

Pineapple Brown Butter

Serves 1

2 tablespoons butter

⅓ cup canned pineapple chunks

2 slices chocolate kuchen bread

½ cup shredded brick cheese

Caramelizing onions is a common practice that adds great flavor to any creation. But this awesomely sweet grilled cheese recipe calls for caramelized butter, which adds a rich, sophisticated, nutty flavor to the sandwich. This technique is less common, but the payoff is well worth it!

1. In a sauté pan, sauté butter on medium heat, whisking until the butter begins to change colors and emits a nutty flavor. Be careful not to burn.
2. Add pineapple to butter, cooking only for a couple of minutes, giving time for the pineapple to be completely covered in the butter.
3. Drain pineapple, saving browned butter liquid.
4. Brush the browned butter on the outside of the 2 slices of bread. In a new, unheated sauté pan, place 1 slice of bread butter side down. Place the pineapple on the bread, followed by the shredded brick cheese. Place other slice of bread on top, butter side up. Turn burner to medium heat.
5. Let sandwich cook for 3–5 minutes per side or until bread is golden brown.
6. Cut on the diagonal and serve warm.

Cinnamon Kiwi

Serves 1

2–4 tablespoons melted sweet butter, for grilling

2 slices cinnamon or chocolate kuchen bread

½ cup shredded Havarti cheese

½–⅔ kiwi, sliced and peeled, depending on taste

½ teaspoon raisins

Caramel syrup, to taste

It's not often that you'll find the kiwi playing a starring role. Perhaps due to its subtle flavor, it usually takes a backseat to stronger players, but not in this recipe! Here, kiwi steps forward to take its rightful place in the spotlight, backed by the sweet tastes of raisins, caramel, and Havarti cheese. This sandwich doubles as a meal or a dessert, so treat yourself to a kiwi delight.

1 Brush the melted butter on the outside of the 2 slices of bread. In an unheated sauté pan, place 1 slice of bread butter side down, followed by the shredded Havarti, kiwi, and raisins. Drizzle, to taste, caramel on top. Place other slice of bread on top, butter side up. Turn burner to medium heat.

2 Let sandwich cook for 3–5 minutes per side or until bread is golden brown.

3 Cut on the diagonal and serve warm.

Carrot Cake

1 box bran bread or muffin mix

¾ cup fresh zucchini, peeled and grated

¼ cup walnuts, divided

3 ounces cream cheese, softened

½ cup fresh carrot, peeled and shredded, divided

2½ teaspoons cinnamon sugar, divided (see Harvest Fest recipe in this chapter for cinnamon sugar details)

With flavors ranging from sweet to nutty, carrot cake is a perennial favorite. This recipe takes all the nutty flavors of the original and packs them into a sweet, creamy grilled cheese! You'll never look at carrot cake the same way again!

❶ Prepare bran bread mix according to instructions on the box, adding ¾ cup zucchini and ⅛ cup walnuts. Bake and cool as directed on box. Cut the loaf in half and slice horizontally.

❷ In a mixing bowl, combine cream cheese, ⅛ cup walnuts, ¼ cup shredded carrot, and 2 teaspoons cinnamon sugar. Spread cream cheese mixture on bottom half of bread, followed by ½ teaspoon cinnamon sugar and ¼ cup shredded carrots. Top with other half of bread.

❸ If desired, place sandwich in oven to warm at 300°F for 5 minutes. Otherwise, serve at room temperature and enjoy.

Carrot Cake

Boston Cream Pie

Boston Cream Pie

Serves 2–4

1 small box instant vanilla pudding

⅛ teaspoon vanilla extract

4 Hostess Shortcakes, scooped (keep dough lids)

4 tablespoons farmers' cheese, divided

Milk chocolate whipped frosting, to cover tops, approximately 1 cup

Powdered sugar, for decoration

A typical Boston Cream Pie is a sponge cake filled with cream, then covered with chocolate. This Boston Cream Pie takes the original recipe and gives it a major flavor boost by adding vanilla custard mixed with farmers' cheese and chocolate whipped frosting. How's that for unbelievable!

❶ Preheat oven to 250°F, or simply use the "warm" setting on your oven.

❷ Prepare instant vanilla pudding according to instructions on box. Add ⅛ teaspoon vanilla extract during preparation.

❸ Place 1 tablespoon farmers' cheese in each shortcake. Bake for 3 minutes. With the back of a spoon, press cheese into cake. Let cool.

❹ Fill each shortcake with ⅛ cup vanilla pudding. Cover with shortcake lids and milk chocolate whipped frosting.

❺ Sprinkle with powdered sugar and serve warm.

Tips from the Stovetop
There will be leftover vanilla pudding that can simply be eaten by itself. Or, you can increase the amount of cheese and shortcakes and use all the vanilla pudding for the Boston Cream Pie.

The Granola Bar

Serves 1

2 tablespoons apple cinnamon granola

2 tablespoons blueberry 'n cream granola

2 tablespoons + 1 tablespoon quark cheese

2–4 tablespoons melted sweet butter, for grilling

2 slices raisin pumpernickel

1 tablespoon cashews, broken

You run to the store—you grab a granola bar. You're rushed for breakfast—granola bar. You need a pick-me-up in the afternoon—granola bar. This quick and easy snack has come through in a pinch more than once, but you can do better! The granola-filled grilled cheese sandwich uses all the flavors that you're used to finding wrapped in that shiny package, but let's be honest, everything is just better when it's included in an amazing grilled cheese.

1 In a bowl, mix apple cinnamon and blueberry 'n cream granola with quark cheese.

2 Brush the melted butter on the outside of the 2 slices of bread. In an unheated sauté pan, place 1 slice of bread butter side down. Spread granola mixture over bread, followed by broken cashews. Place other slice of bread on top, butter side up. Turn burner to medium heat.

3 Let sandwich cook on medium heat for 3–5 minutes per side or until bread is golden brown.

4 Cut on the diagonal and serve warm.

Tips from the Stovetop

There are many, many different varieties of granola; each type contains different seasonings and fruits. Mix and match for various flavors and combinations. Buying in bulk is a great way to get started as you experiment with granola.

Sweet Grapes and Brie

2–4 tablespoons sweet butter

½ cup fresh, seedless green grapes, halved

1½ tablespoons white sugar

1 tablespoon brown sugar

½ cup water

Salt and pepper to taste

1 Italian sesame roll (hoagie bun), sliced horizontally

Approximately ½, small wheel, approximately 12", of Brie, enough to cover bread

The flavors of the grapes and Brie meld into one amazing taste when placed between two crunchy halves of Italian sesame bread. The mixture of the sweet grapes and creamy texture of the Brie provide for a unique eating experience. Add the Italian bread, which is mild enough to allow the sweet flavors to seep through, and you have yourself an unexpected but wonderful grilled cheese sandwich.

1. In a sauté pan, melt sweet butter over medium heat. Add grapes, white and brown sugar, water, and salt and pepper, to taste. Cook until grapes soften, approximately 7–10 minutes. Drain sweetened grapes, saving the liquid.
2. Preheat oven to 350°F.
3. Drizzle grape liquid over the bottom half of the roll. Spread Brie over bread, followed by sweetened grapes and the other half of bread.
4. Bake for 5–7 minutes and serve warm.

Chocolate Mascarpone and Strawberry

Serves 1

¼ cup mascarpone cheese

5–6 chocolate discs, melted, divided

2–4 tablespoons melted sweet butter, for grilling

2 slices brioche bread, hand-cut

2–3 graham crackers, broken into small–medium pieces

4–5 fresh strawberries, sliced

If you have been tasked with preparing a dessert for a romantic dinner, this sandwich is the perfect option. Filled with the foods of romance—chocolate, mascarpone, and strawberries—this recipe brings a little bit of ooh-la-la to any table. The fact that it's a sweet grilled cheese sandwich is just the cherry on top!

❶ In a bowl, mix mascarpone and ½ of the melted chocolate.

❷ Brush 2–4 tablespoons melted butter on the outside of the 2 slices of bread. In a sauté pan, brown outside of bread over medium heat for 1–2 minutes. Set on serving dish. Spread chocolate mascarpone on bread, followed by broken graham crackers, sliced strawberries, and ½ of remaining drizzled chocolate. Close sandwich with other piece of challah, cooked side up.

❸ Drizzle remaining melted chocolate over top of sandwich. Serve at room temperature.

Chocolate Mascarpone and Strawberry

Strawberry-Mango

Serves 1

8 strawberries, sliced, divided

½ mango, sliced, divided

1½ tablespoons olive oil

Salt, to taste

2–4 tablespoons melted sweet butter, for grilling

2 slices pumpernickel bread

½ cup shredded Gouda

This recipe uses fruit in two different—but extraordinarily complementary—ways! This grilled cheese is packed with a fruit salsa, a partially juiced mashup of various fruits that really allows the flavors to mingle, and fresh fruit slices that keep the crunch alive! This recipe's satisfactory sweet flavor doesn't overpower and never disappoints. Guaranteed!

1. In a blender, mix on high half of the sliced strawberries and mangoes, olive oil, and salt into a fine liquid. Set aside.
2. Brush 2–4 tablespoons melted butter on the outside of the 2 slices of bread. In an unheated sauté pan, place 1 slice of bread butter side down. Spread half of the fruit mixture on the bread, followed by the shredded Gouda, sliced strawberries, sliced mangoes, and the rest of the fruit mixture. Place the other slice of bread on top, butter side up. Turn burner to medium heat.
3. Let sandwich cook for 3–5 minutes per side or until bread is golden brown.
4. Cut on the diagonal and serve warm.

Tips from the Stovetop

Strawberries and mangoes are simply options when creating a fruit salsa such as this. Feel free to sub in pineapple, blueberries, and even kiwi if you'd prefer.

Chapter 4

Experimental Territory

Just because a grilled cheese sandwich is sweet doesn't mean that it can't push some serious culinary boundaries. Today, restaurants and food trucks have thought outside the box and created some amazing, distinctive treats. The sweet recipes in this chapter take inspiration from those grilled cheese gurus and showcase experimentally delicious gourmet concoctions. White bread has been tossed aside in favor of unexpected goodies like brownies, cookies, and Rice Krispies treats. Here, Camembert, crème fraîche, and mascarpone are finally getting their due. These exceptional ingredients provide something for everyone and give you a jumping-off point for your own experimental adventures into the world of sweet grilled cheese sandwiches. Get ready to try something new!

Dessert Waffles

Serves 1

3 ounces blueberries, or your favorite fruit

1½ tablespoons sugar

⅓ cup farmers' cheese

2 waffles cooked

Waffles make a perfect breakfast dish, but rather than serving them the same old way, time after time, use them to create an exceptional grilled cheese! Feel free to give these sandwiches—which are also perfect for dessert—your own unique spin by adding your favorite fruit to the mix.

1. Preheat oven to 350°F.
2. Softly fold the blueberries and sugar into the farmers' cheese and place most of the mixture on 1 waffle, leaving only a large spoonful behind. Place other waffle on top.
3. Bake for 5 minutes on a baking sheet.
4. Place remaining farmers' cheese mixture on top and serve warm.

Cheerios and Honey

2–4 tablespoons melted sweet butter, for grilling

2 slices multigrain or banana bread

⅓ banana, sliced

¼ cup Cheerios

⅛ cup slivered almonds

Honey, to taste

½ cup Jarlsberg cheese shredded

Cheerios are one of America's favorite breakfast foods, but why limit this healthy cereal to breakfast? Turns out that these crunchy Os pair perfectly with cheese, almonds, and bananas to create a grilled cheese that's perfect for breakfast, lunch, dinner, or whenever you feel like working some magic in the kitchen!

1. Brush the melted butter on the outside of the 2 slices of bread. In an unheated sauté pan, place 1 slice of bread butter side down, followed by the sliced banana, Cheerios, slivered almonds, honey, and Jarlsberg cheese. Place other slice of bread on top, butter side up. Turn burner to medium heat.
2. Let sandwich cook for 5 minutes per side or until bread is golden brown.
3. Cut on the diagonal and serve warm.

Tips from the Stovetop

Want to add your own personal flair? Change up the flavor of your sandwich by using different varieties of Cheerios.

Stuffed French Toast

Stuffed French Toast

You have really never had French Toast until you have had challah French Toast! This traditional egg bread adds the perfect amount of sweetness to take this grilled cheese from good to amazing. The flavors of the fresh fruit layer over the sweetness of the challah send this sandwich over the top.

FOR STUFFING

¼ cup fresh raspberries

1 teaspoon sugar

¼ cup + 1 tablespoon farmers' cheese

FOR FRENCH TOAST BATTER

1 jumbo egg

⅓ cup milk

2 teaspoons cinnamon sugar (see Harvest Fest recipe in Chapter 3 for cinnamon sugar details)

Drop of vanilla extract

FOR STUFFED FRENCH TOAST

1–2 tablespoons sweet butter

2 hand-cut slices challah

Cinnamon sugar, to taste

Powdered sugar, for decoration

1. In a mixing bowl, mix with a fork the egg, milk, and cinnamon sugar to create batter. Set aside.

2. In a separate mixing bowl, combine fresh raspberries and sugar. Softly mix in the farmers' cheese, being careful not to break the raspberries. Set aside.

3. Warm sauté pan to medium heat and melt 1–2 tablespoons of butter. Dredge both slices of the challah in batter. Place slices in pan and brown on both sides, approximately 5 minutes. When flipping challah, sprinkle with cinnamon sugar to taste. Take off heat and spread farmers' cheese mixture on 1 slice, leaving a spoonful behind. Place other slice of bread on top.

4. Place remaining farmers' cheese mixture on top of bread, sprinkle with powdered sugar, and serve warm.

Tips from the Stovetop

Raspberries are not the only fruit option for this Stuffed French Toast. If you want to mix it up, try including strawberries, blackberries, blueberries, or peaches. You can try them separately or do your own experiment and mix them together to create different flavors.

The Candied Baconator

Serves 1

- ½ cup dark brown sugar
- 4–5 slices thick-cut bacon
- ½ cup ricotta cheese
- 4–5 caramel chews, diced or torn into small pieces
- ½ teaspoon vanilla extract
- 2–4 tablespoons melted sweet butter, for grilling
- 2 slices sweet brioche bread

This guest recipe is the ultimate sweet bacon treat. It may sound strange, but you'll find that the sweet and salty interplay of the candied bacon actually gives this sandwich complex layers of flavor that make it perfect for entertaining!

1. Preheat an oven to 350°F degrees. While the oven is warming, spread the brown sugar out in a shallow bowl, and toss the bacon with it until the bacon is fully coated. Place the sugared bacon onto a foil-lined bacon sheet, and into the oven.
2. Bake the candied bacon for 20–30 minutes, depending on the thickness of your bacon. The sugar should be fully melted and the bacon should be brown. Transfer the bacon to wax paper to cool, but be careful of the hot sugar.
3. In a small bowl, combine the ricotta cheese, the caramel pieces, and the vanilla extract, and mix them together just until combined.
4. Brush the melted butter on the outside of the 2 slices of brioche. In an unheated sauté pan, place 1 slice of bread butter side down.
5. Layer the brioche with the sweet ricotta mixture and the cooled candied bacon. Top the sandwich with the other slice of buttered brioche. Turn burner to medium heat.
6. Let sandwich cook for 3–5 minutes per side or until bread is golden brown.
7. Cut on the diagonal and serve at room temperature.

Rice Krispies Treats

Serves 1

1 large Rice Krispies treat

Brie to cover 1 side of Rice Krispies treat

Peanut butter to cover 1 side of Rice Krispies treat

7 chocolate discs, melted

Rice Krispies Treats may be a blast from the past, but there's no reason to leave this great snack to languish in children's lunchboxes. This recipe puts the Rice Krispies Treat front and center by using it as the bread for the grilled cheese. This sandwich is still good for kids, but it's probably more appropriate for a dessert after a great, grown-up meal. Lucky you!

1. Preheat oven to 250°F.
2. Cut the Rice Krispies treat horizontally. Spread brie on 1 half and peanut butter on the other. Drizzle melted chocolate on the peanut butter side.
3. Place only the brie half on a baking sheet and in the oven for 3 minutes. Set aside.
4. Combine the covered sides.
5. Cut in half and serve.

Tips from the Stovetop

You are able to purchase pre-made large Rice Krispies Treats at stores like Einstein Bros Bagels and Dollar Tree, among other local establishments. You can also purchase a box of Rice Krispies Treats from the grocery store and combine two small ones, making one large one. Or you can harken back to your childhood and make your own. The recipe's easy and you know your treats will be fresh.

Coffee Sponge Cake

Serves 1

3 ounces cream cheese

3 teaspoons cinnamon sugar, divided (see Harvest Fest recipe in Chapter 3 for cinnamon sugar details)

½ teaspoon vanilla

2–4 tablespoons melted sweet butter, for grilling

2 hand-cut slices challah

¼ teaspoon instant coffee granules

6 chocolate chip morsels, melted

The only thing better than a sweet grilled cheese is one that comes packed full of get-up-and-go. Leave your coffee cup at home, because this recipe is packed full of everyone's favorite shot of caffeine. And as if the rich coffee wasn't enough for you, this sandwich also contains plenty of cinnamon and sugar. It's like a cup of Joe and a delicious Danish . . . all in the palm of your hand.

1 In a mixing bowl, combine cream cheese, 2 teaspoons cinnamon sugar, and vanilla. Set aside.

2 Brush the melted butter on the outside of the 2 slices of bread. Sprinkle each slice of bread with the remaining 1 teaspoon of cinnamon sugar. In a sauté pan, place 1 slice of bread butter side down. Place cream cheese mixture on bread. Sprinkle coffee grounds on top and drizzle with melted chocolate. Place other slice of bread on top, butter side up.

3 Let sandwich cook on medium heat for 3–5 minutes per side or until bread is golden brown.

4 Cut on the diagonal and serve warm.

The S'more

Serves 1

2 graham crackers

½ cup crumbled Raclette cheese

1–2 tablespoons crème fraîche

2 large marshmallows, sliced in half

8 chocolate discs, melted

S'mores are a campfire classic, but you're a grown-up who's looking for a grilled cheese with a grown-up sensibility. Enter The S'more! This particular sandwich doesn't require a campfire—just imagination and a deep love for chocolate. Feel free to throw in a ghost story or two to set the mood!

❶ Preheat oven to 325°F.

❷ On top of 1 graham cracker, place the Raclette cheese, crème fraîche, and marshmallows. Drizzle the melted chocolate on top of the marshmallows. Top with other graham cracker and bake for 3–5 minutes on a baking pan.

❸ Let newly created S'mores sandwich cool for 3 minutes, allowing the cheese to coagulate. Eat and enjoy.

Tips from the Stovetop

The crème fraîche and Raclette cheese will run, so this S'more will be messy. But it is most definitely worth the effort. Just make sure to have napkins nearby and you will be all set.

Chocolate Brownie Indulgence

2 brownies measured 5" square

¼ cup mascarpone

1 chocolate sandwich cookie, crumbled

1 teaspoon gourmet hot fudge

Powdered sugar, for decoration

If you love chocolate—really, truly, passionately love chocolate—then the Chocolate Brownie Indulgence is the right treat for you! With its combination of chocolate brownies, chocolate sandwich cookies, and rich hot fudge, this over-the-top grilled cheese sandwich is the perfect dessert for any chocoholic . . . or you could just skip dinner and go right for the good stuff.

❶ Preheat oven to 350°F.

❷ Spread mascarpone over one brownie, followed by crumbled chocolate sandwich cookie and hot fudge. Close sandwich with other half of brownie.

❸ Bake for 6 minutes on a baking sheet.

❹ Sprinkle with powdered sugar for decoration and serve warm.

Chocolate Brownie Indulgence

Crème de Menthe

Serves 1

1 teaspoon crème de menthe liqueur

3 ounces cream cheese, softened

1 multigrain or plain English muffin

1 tablespoon chocolate chips

Maybe you've had crème de menthe in a glass on the rocks, but this recipe takes this after-dinner liqueur somewhere it's never gone before: the grilled cheese sandwich. Surprisingly, the liqueur's smooth and creamy texture and mint flavor pair seamlessly with the cream cheese and chocolate chips, turning this after-dinner treat into a perfect midnight snack.

❶ Mix crème de menthe and softened cream cheese in a bowl.

❷ Spread cream cheese mixture on bottom of English muffin. Sprinkle chocolate chips on top. Close sandwich with other half of English muffin.

❸ Bake at 325°F for 3 minutes and serve warm.

Tips from the Stovetop
Liqueur is an alcoholic beverage bottled with sugars. It may consist of a variety of ingredients, such as fruit, herbs, nuts, spices, flowers, or cream. Note that in this recipe, the liqueur isn't heated long enough for the alcohol to burn off—so don't eat and drive.

Noodle Pudding

Noodle Pudding, also known as Noodle Kugel, is an old European dish often served at holidays and family gatherings. This casserole-like dish includes the sweet flavors of fruit, raisins, and cinnamon as well as egg noodles. Mix it all together and take this Old World tradition to a modern level by adding crème fraiche cheese and wrapping it all between two slices of cinnamon bread.

FOR PUDDING

3 cups water

2 cups wide egg noodles

1 jumbo egg

3 tablespoons margarine, divided

⅛ cup white sugar

2 tablespoons + ½ teaspoon cinnamon sugar (see Harvest Fest recipe in Chapter 3 for cinnamon sugar details)

1 tablespoon brown sugar

1 teaspoon vanilla

½ cup canned, sliced peaches

3 tablespoons canned peach juice

⅛ cup raisins

FOR SANDWICH

4–6 tablespoons melted sweet butter, for grilling

4 slices cinnamon bread

½ cup crème fraîche, divided

1. Boil water in a saucepan. Add noodles to water, boiling until soft, approximately 8–10 minutes. Drain noodles.
2. Preheat oven to 375°F.
3. Combine and mix following ingredients with boiled noodles: egg, 2 tablespoons of margarine, white sugar, 2 tablespoons cinnamon sugar, vanilla, brown sugar, peaches, peach juice, and raisins.
4. Pour into greased baking dish. Sprinkle with ½ teaspoon cinnamon sugar and evenly distribute remaining tablespoon of margarine.
5. Bake for 35 minutes, or until top becomes brown. Set aside to cool. When cool, slice in half.
6. Brush melted butter on the outside of the 4 slices of bread. In a sauté pan, place 2 slices of bread butter side down. Place each "slice" of noodle pudding on each slice of bread, followed by ¼ cup crème fraîche per sandwich. Place the other 2 slices of bread on top, butter side up.
7. Let sandwiches cook on medium heat for 5 minutes per side or until bread is golden brown.
8. Cut on the diagonal and serve warm.

The Cinnamon Roll

The Cinnamon Roll

Serves 1

1 package refrigerated Pillsbury Cinnamon Rolls with Icing

¼ cup Philadelphia Indulgence Milk Chocolate cream cheese spread

¼ teaspoon cinnamon sugar (see Harvest Fest recipe in Chapter 3 for cinnamon sugar details)

Caramelized pecans, to taste (optional)

If you're yearning for something sweet and sticky, search no further than the cinnamon roll! This grilled cheese pushes the envelope and uses these sticky treats as the base upon which the pecans, cinnamon, and milk chocolate cream cheese are spread.

❶ Preheat oven to 375°F.

❷ Remove icing from package and set aside.

❸ Take 3 cinnamon rolls out of package and place in a circle on a greased baking pan. Unwrap the cinnamon rolls, combining the creases and turning them into a single large cinnamon roll.

❹ Spread milk chocolate cream cheese spread on cinnamon roll and sprinkle cinnamon sugar on top. Bake for 15 minutes, or until golden brown.

❺ Remove from oven and cool for 5–10 minutes. Once cool to the touch, gently spread desired amount of icing from container on top of cream cheese spread. Crush caramelized pecans on top, if desired. Serve warm.

Tips from the Stovetop

If you cannot find Philadelphia Indulgence cream cheese spread at your local grocery store, simply melt any type of chocolate and mix with regular cream cheese.

Cookie Cheesecake

Serves 1

3 ounces cream cheese

2–3 tablespoons of 1 beaten egg

2 tablespoons sugar

1 teaspoon vanilla

2 large chocolate chip cookies

3 strawberries, sliced

1 tablespoon powdered sugar

This extremely rich cookie cheesecake is not for the dessert novice. This sandwich creates a uniquely sweet profile that is highlighted by the addition of fresh strawberries. Be prepared for many sweet and rich flavors combining to create a smooth texture that has you wanting more.

❶ Preheat oven to 325°F.

❷ In a mixing bowl, combine cream cheese, egg, sugar, and vanilla. Carefully place this cheesecake mixture on 1 chocolate chip cookie, top side down. It may overflow. Mix strawberries with powdered sugar and place on top of mixture. Set second cookie aside.

❸ Bake covered cookie for 12 minutes. Remove from oven and place in refrigerator for 10–15 minutes, allowing the cheesecake mixture to set.

❹ Remove from refrigerator and top with second cookie, bottom side down. Sprinkle more powdered sugar on top if desired. Serve at room temperature.

Cookie Cheesecake

Mascarpone Pound Cake

Mascarpone Pound Cake

Serves 1

1 tablespoon sweet butter

1 banana, sliced

2 tablespoons flaked coconut

½ tablespoon brown sugar

½ teaspoon crème de cacao liqueur

2 slices pound cake

¼ cup mascarpone

Pound cake is normally served as a dessert, typically with a fruit topping. In this recipe however, pound cake breaks out of its normal ho-hum role and serves as the bread for this sweet grilled cheese sandwich. And, when it really comes right down to it, what else would you want holding in the tropical flavors of banana and coconut?

❶ In a sauté pan, cook, on medium heat, sweet butter, banana, flaked coconut, brown sugar, and crème de cacao until a syrup appears, approximately 5 minutes. Once done, remove from heat and refrigerate for 10 minutes, allowing mixture to set.

❷ Preheat oven to 350°F.

❸ On the bottom slice of pound cake, spread the mascarpone, followed by the banana mixture. Top with the other slice of pound cake.

❹ Bake for 5 minutes on a baking sheet, remove from oven, and serve warm.

Cherries Jubilee

Serves 1

1 cup cherry pie filling

¼ cup brandy liqueur

1 package Pillsbury Crescent Rolls

2.33 ounces Camembert (⅓ of a small wheel)

Traditional Cherries Jubilee requires a time-intensive process involving liqueur and an open flame. This recipe takes the flavors of this classic dessert and inserts them into an easy-to-make grilled cheese. Here, the cherries are mixed with Camembert cheese to create the sweet, tangy flavor that's synonymous with a jubilee and, while the open flame has been taken out of the equation, the brandy remains to help create a unique dessert that will get your guests talking.

1. Preheat oven to 350°F.
2. In a sauté pan, cook cherry pie filling and brandy liqueur over medium heat until warm.
3. In an au gratin plate, lay out 2 crescent rolls and press edges together to make a rectangle. Cover with Camembert and cherry pie mixture.
4. Bake for 12 minutes and serve hot.

Cherries Jubilee

Amaretto Rhubarb

With its bitter flavor, rhubarb makes ideal company for sugar, which transforms this tart vegetable into a sweet and savory ingredient. The nutty flavor of amaretto blended with the tanginess of rhubarb creates a sophisticated presentation atop muffin tops.

FOR RHUBARB MIXTURE

⅔ cup water

2 stalks fresh rhubarb

⅓ cup sugar

¼ cup applesauce

1 teaspoon amaretto liqueur

FOR SANDWICH

2 lemon poppyseed muffin tops

¼ cup quark cheese

❶ Boil water over medium heat. Break up rhubarb into medium-sized pieces, approximately 2" long and add to water. With a fork, continuously stir until rhubarb has a string-like consistency, approximately 7–10 minutes. Add sugar and applesauce. Reduce to simmer and cook until rhubarb thickens. Cool and then strain excess liquid. Add amaretto liqueur.

❷ Preheat oven to 225°F.

❸ Spread rhubarb over 1 muffin top, followed by quark cheese and other muffin top.

❹ Bake for 3 minutes on baking sheet, remove from oven, and serve warm.

The Snack Time

⅛ cup M&M's

1 gluten-free demi-baguette, scooped

⅓ cup Pirate's Booty Aged White Cheddar

10 gluten-free pretzel sticks

2 string cheese sticks, separated

1 tablespoon melted sweet butter

This gluten-free grilled cheese gives even those with gluten intolerance a seat at the table! If you do have a gluten sensitivity, when cooking, make sure not to cross-contaminate the ingredients for this sandwich with any gluten ingredients or cooking utensils. If you are able to enjoy gluten-filled products, feel free to sub in your favorite brands for the gluten-free ingredients given here.

1 Preheat oven to 350°F.

2 Crush the M&M's with a mortar and pestle (or the handle of a knife), creating a crunchy substance.

3 Layer the baguette with the Pirate's Booty, pretzel sticks, cheese sticks, and crushed M&M's. Then brush sweet butter on outside of the bread.

4 Bake for 5 minutes on a baking sheet. Remove from oven and serve warm.

Tips from the Stovetop

Gluten-free breads and ingredient options are appearing more and more in many grocery stores and can be found in the freezer or fresh bread department. Whole Foods, among other chains, provides a great variety of options for the gluten intolerant.

Crunchy Chocolate Peanut

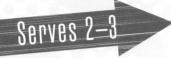

Serves 2–3

1 can Pillsbury Crescent Recipe
   Creations refrigerated seamless
   dough sheet, or 1 pie crust

8 chocolate discs

3.5 ounces Camembert (½ of a
   small wheel)

1 cup Chocolate Nut Crunch (found
   at Whole Foods Market)

1 beaten egg, for egg wash

If you feel that chocolate and peanut butter should always be served together, then this sandwich pocket is perfect for you! If you're looking for larger portions and a more intense chocolate/nut flavor, cut the dough in half as opposed to thirds.

❶ Preheat oven to 350°F.

❷ Melt chocolate discs and set aside.

❸ Assemble the following creation on greased baking sheet. Roll out dough and cut 3 rectangles. Spread Camembert and Chocolate Nut Crunch over the bottom half of each dough rectangle.

❹ Close the pocket by taking one end of the rectangle and wrapping it over the chocolate and Camembert. Seal edges, cutting off any excess dough.

❺ Brush egg wash on top of the pockets. Bake for 15 minutes.

❻ Remove from oven and immediately drizzle melted chocolate over the pockets. Serve hot.

Tips from the Stovetop

Chocolate Nut Crunch is available in the bulk department of certain Whole Foods Markets. However, if you're feeling ambitious, try making your own Chocolate Nut Crunch. Included in this mixture are roasted almonds, roasted peanuts, chocolate chips, peanut butter raisins, raisins, peanut butter chips, chocolate chips, chocolate stars, and chocolate peanuts. Combine ingredients in equal parts or vary to personal preferences.

The Twisted Parfait

½ cup shredded yogurt cheese

6 ounces Wallaby Organic Orange Passion Fruit yogurt

1 large waffle cone

6 segments fresh orange, cut in thirds, resulting in 18 orange pieces

12 whole blackberries

When you typically think of a grilled cheese, you think of a sandwich that's actually been, you know, grilled. Well, this recipe turns that idea on its head! In this recipe, the ingredients are served cold, in a parfait glass. So does this still count as a grilled cheese? If you're thinking out of the box, the answer is a resounding yes!

1. In a small bowl, mix yogurt cheese and yogurt.
2. Divide 3 of the blackberries in half. Set aside.
3. In the bottom of waffle cone, place 1 piece of orange, followed by 2 ounces of yogurt mixture. Then layer the following on top of it: 4 pieces of oranges, 6 blackberry halves, 1 ounce of yogurt mixture to cover fruit, 3 whole blackberries, 5 orange pieces, and the remainder of the yogurt mixture. Top with 6 whole blackberries covered with 8 orange pieces.
4. Serve cold in a parfait glass with a spoon.

Sea Salt Caramel

⅓ cup mascarpone cheese

6 squares Jelina Chocolatier/
Galerie au Chocolate Sea Salt/
Fleur de Sel Chocolate, 5 melted,
1 shaven

8 Nestlé Toll House Swirled Milk
Chocolate & Caramel Morsels

Fresh cracked sea salt, to taste

2 palmier cookies

Caramel syrup, to taste

Once upon a time, sea salt and chocolate seemed like a crazy idea. "Who puts salt in chocolate?" Now, it is ubiquitous and has most often been paired with caramel. One would expect the combination of these flavors to clash; however, the opposite is true . . . creating a unified explosion in your mouth.

❶ Preheat oven to 325°F.

❷ Mix mascarpone cheese with melted sea salt chocolates, whole chocolate & caramel morsels, and fresh cracked sea salt, to taste. Spread over the bottom of 1 palmier cookie. Drizzle caramel, to taste, half of the chocolate shavings, and more fresh cracked sea salt, to taste.

❸ Bake for 2 minutes on a baking sheet.

❹ Cover with other cookie, drizzle with more caramel and remaining chocolate shavings, and serve warm.

Tips from the Stovetop
If you cannot find Jelina Chocolatier chocolate bars in your neighborhood, feel free to substitute other high-quality sea salt chocolate bars.

Pumpkin Pie

Serves 2

½ store-bought 8" pumpkin pie, or 2 cups pumpkin pie filling

3 tablespoons cream cheese

1 tablespoon cinnamon

1 tablespoon cinnamon sugar (see Harvest Fest recipe in Chapter 3 for cinnamon sugar details)

4–6 tablespoons melted sweet butter, for grilling

4 slices cracked wheat bread, or brioche

1 cup gorgonzola cheese, divided

Gorgonzola cheese, pumpkin pie, and cream cheese may not seem like complementing ingredients, but after you taste this sandwich, you'll have a new appreciation for this totally awesome triumvirate. The addition of the gorgonzola cheese adds a complementary kick to the sweet pumpkin pie while the cream cheese incorporates a cooling effect.

1 Scoop filling out of half of pumpkin pie, leaving the crust behind.

2 In a mixing bowl, combine pumpkin pie with cream cheese, cinnamon, and cinnamon sugar. Set aside.

3 Brush melted butter on the outside of the 4 slices of bread. In a sauté pan, place 2 slices of bread butter side down. Spread ½ of the pumpkin mixture on each slice of bread, followed by ½ cup of gorgonzola cheese per sandwich. Place the other 2 slices of bread on top, butter side up.

4 Let sandwiches cook on medium heat for 5 minutes per side or until bread is golden brown.

5 Cut on the diagonal and serve warm.

The Candy Cane

Serves 2–4

1 can Pillsbury Grands! Jr. Golden
Layers refrigerated biscuits

⅛ cup crushed peppermint candies
or candy canes

½ cup ricotta cheese

4 gingersnap cookies, cracked into
pea-sized chunks

Around the holidays it seems that everyone is looking for the next peppermint treat. Surprise your guests with this holly, jolly grilled cheese recipe. While these have been created as party sandwiches, you can enjoy them even if your party totals just one!

1. Bake 4 biscuits according to instructions on packaging. Let cool and then slice horizontally.
2. Preheat oven to 350°F.
3. In a mixing bowl, combine crushed peppermint and ricotta cheese.
4. Distribute gingersnap chunks evenly on bottom half of each biscuit, followed by ricotta/peppermint mixture and top of biscuits.
5. Bake for 3 minutes on a baking sheet, remove from oven, and serve warm.

Tips from the Stovetop
If you'd like, replace gingersnap cookies with gingerbread cookies to make this grilled cheese sandwich even more festive!

Suitable Substitutions

As you've looked through the recipes you may have seem some cheeses and breads that looked a little off the beaten path. While you're ready to take your grilled cheese to the max, for days when you're not feeling all that daring, or if you just can't find a particular bread or cheese at your local supermarket, here are some suitable substitutions.

BREADS

In Recipe	Flavor Profile	Suitable Substitute
(chocolate) kuchen bread	sweet, gooey, rich	cinnamon bread
sunflower bread	salty, nutty, earth	harvest whole wheat or multigrain/seven grain
rosemary bread	sweet, pungent, pine-like fragrance	Italian bread
ciabatta rolls	crusty, dense, tangy	rustic roll, sourdough
Tuscany bread	neutral, undistinctive, flat	Italian bread
pugliese bread	crusty, dense	Italian or ciabatta

CHEESES

In Recipe	Flavor Profile	Suitable Substitute
quark cheese	fresh, mild, creamy	sour cream or ricotta
Raclette cheese	strong, aromatic, nutty	Gruyere or Emmentaler
Chaumes cheese	soft, creamy, rich, full-bodied, hazelnut aftertaste	Muenster
Chihuahua cheese	salty, creamy, mild	jack or mild/medium cheddar
marble cheese	mild, moist, creamy	Colby
Manchego cheese	sharp, buttery, nutty	Parmigiano Reggiano
Dubliner cheese	sharp, nutty, robust	extra sharp Cheddar
Cantalet cheese	buttery, nutty, earthy undertones	farmhouse/sharp Cheddar

Index

Ahi Tuna Steak Melt, 22
Amaretto Rhubarb, 148
Apples. *See* Fruit
Asparagus and Lemon Pepper Vinaigrette, 50–51

Bacon Filet, The 47
Balsamic Basil, 15
Basil
    Balsamic Basil, 15
    Basil Peppercorn, 16–17
BBQ Chickpeas, 38
Beans and legumes
    BBQ Chickpeas, 38
    Pretzel Baked Beans, 82–83
    Quinoa Black Bean, 33
    Sea Salt Hummus, 60
Beer, Kale, and Crouton Mash-Up, The 64
Berries. *See* Fruit
Blue Potato, 32
Boston Cream Pie, 120–21
Bread substitutions, 157
Broccoli Alfredo, 69

Candied Baconator, The 132
Candy Cane, The 154–55
Caprese, Updated, 24–25
Carrot Cake, 118–19
Cayenne Cornbread, 44–45
Cheerios and Honey, 129
Cheese, types of, 10–11, 157
Cherries Jubilee, 146–47
Chips
    Big Game Nachos and Cheese, 98
    Stuffed Chips, 76
Chocolate
    Chocolate Brownie Indulgence, 136–37
    Chocolate Mascarpone and Strawberry, 124–25
    Crunchy Chocolate Peanut, 150
    Sea Salt Caramel, 152
    S'more, The 135
Ciliegine with Lime Vinaigrette, 40–41

Cinnamon Kiwi, 117
Cinnamon Roll, The 140–41
Citrus sauces. *See* Sauces and spreads
Classic Meatballs Marinara, 20
Coconut Peach, 108
Coffee Sponge Cake, 134
Cookie Cheesecake, 142–43
Cooking grilled cheese, 10–11
Corn. *See also* Chips
    Cayenne Cornbread, 44–45
    Spicy Soy, The 42
    Sweet and Spicy Popcorn, 55
Crème de Menthe, 138
Crème Fraîche with Apple and Cucumber, 30–31
Currant Jam, 112
Curried Egg Salad, 23

Deconstructed, The 54
Desserts. *See* Chocolate; Fruit; Sweet stacks
Double Decker, The 68

Eggplant sliders (mini), 96–97
Eggs
    Curried Egg Salad, 23
    Fried Egg, The 46
    Fried Matzoh with Horseradish Mayo, 90
    Stuffed French Toast, 131
    Sunday Brunch, The 34–35

Farfalle Pesto Grilled Cheese, 74–75
Fish
    Ahi Tuna Steak Melt, 22
    Fish 'N Chips, 58–59
    Fusion Salmon Piccata, 21
    Salmon Croquettes with Dill, 48–49
    Unusual Reuben, The 57
French toast, stuffed, 131
Fried Egg, The 46
Fried Matzoh with Horseradish Mayo, 90
Fruit
    Amaretto Rhubarb, 148
    Apple Pie, 114–15
    Cherries Jubilee, 146–47

    Chocolate Mascarpone and Strawberry, 124–25
    Cinnamon Kiwi, 117
    Coconut Peach, 108
    Crème Fraîche with Apple and Cucumber, 30–31
    Currant Jam, 112
    Marinated Berries, 106–7
    Pineapple Brown Butter, 116
    Strawberry-Mango, 126
    Stuffed French Toast, 131
    Sweet Grapes and Brie, 123
    Tropical, The 110–11
    Twisted Parfait, The 151
    Walnut Pomegranate, 113
Fusion Salmon Piccata, 21

Garlic. *See* Onions and garlic
Grains
    The Granola Bar, 122
    Quinoa Black Bean, 33
    Rice Krispies Treats, 133
    Risotto, 66–67
Green Tea Tofu, 61

Harvest Fest, 102–3
Hashbrown, The 88–89
Homemade Salsa, 52
Honey Roasted PB & J, 104

Inside-Out Blue Cheese Pecan, 77

Kicked-Up Mint, 109

Marinated Berries, 106–7
Mascarpone Pound Cake, 144–45
Meat
    The Bacon Filet, 47
    Boneless Buffalo Wings, 87
    The Candied Baconator, 132
    Classic Meatballs Marinara, 20
    Prosciutto and Arugula, 28
Mediterranean, The 27

Mint
Candy Cane, The 154–55
Crème de Menthe, 138
Kicked-Up Mint, 109
Mushrooms
Double Decker, The 68
Stuffed Mushrooms, 70–71
White Wine and Mushrooms, 37

Noodles. *See* Pasta
Nuts and seeds
Crunchy Chocolate Peanut, 150
Honey Roasted PB & J, 104
Inside-Out Blue Cheese Pecan, 77
Nutella, The 101
Pistachio and Beets, 18–19
Sunflower Gouda Griller, 36
Walnut Pomegranate, 113

Onions and garlic
Basil Peppercorn, 16–17
Deconstructed, The 54
Garlic and Green Onion Mashed Potato, 91
Oh! Rings, 72–73
Roasted Garlic Tomato Aioli, 39
Soup-less French Onion, 26
Stuffed Chips, 76
Sunday Brunch, The 34–35

Pasta
Farfalle Pesto Grilled Cheese, 74–75
Noodle Pudding, 139
Pineapple Brown Butter, 116
Pistachio and Beets, 18–19
Pizza Volcano, The 86
Potatoes
Blue Potato, The 32
Garlic and Green Onion Mashed Potato, 91
Harvest Fest (sweet potatoes), 102–3
Hashbrown, The 88–89
Potato Pancake, The 92–93
Ultimate Cheesy Fries, 80–81
Pretzel Baked Beans, 82–83
Prosciutto and Arugula, 28
Pumpkin Pie, 153

Quinoa Black Bean, 33

Ramen, The 62–63
Rice. *See* Grains
Risotto, 66–67
Roasted Brussels Sprouts with Cheddar, 29
Roasted Garlic Tomato Aioli, 39

Salmon. *See* Fish
Sauces and spreads
Homemade Salsa, 52
Horseradish Mayo, 90
Lemon Dill Mayonnaise, 49
Lemon Pepper Vinaigrette, 50
Lime Vinaigrette, 41
Mustard Spread, 43
Roasted Garlic Tomato Aioli, 39
Scrambled Spanakopita, The 84–85
Sea Salt Caramel, 152
Sea Salt Hummus, 60
S'more, The 135
Snack Time, The 149
Soup-less French Onion, 26
Spicy Dubliner, The 94–95
Spicy Soy, The 42
Squash with Apple Butter, 105
Stuffed French Toast, 131
Stuffed Mushrooms, 70–71
Substitutions, 156–57
Sunday Brunch, 34–35
Sunflower Gouda Griller, 36
Sweet and Spicy Popcorn, 55
Sweet stacks. *See also* Chocolate; Fruit
Boston Cream Pie, 120–21
Candied Baconator, The 132
Candy Cane, The 154–55
Carrot Cake, 118–19
Cheerios and Honey, 129
Cinnamon Roll, The 140–41
Coffee Sponge Cake, 134
Cookie Cheesecake, 142–43
Crème de Menthe, 138
Dessert Waffles, 128
Granola Bar, The 122
Harvest Fest, 102–3
Honey Roasted PB & J, 104
Kicked-Up Mint, 109
Mascarpone Pound Cake, 144–45
Noodle Pudding, 139

Nutella, The 101
Pumpkin Pie, 153
Rice Krispies Treats, 133
Snack Time, The 149
Squash with Apple Butter, 105

Tillamook Cheddar and Baby Bok Choy, 43
Tofu, in Green Tea Tofu, 61
Tropical, The 110–11
Twisted Parfait, The 151

Ultimate Cheesy Fries, 80–81
Unusual Reuben, The 57

Veggies and tomatoes. *See also* Onions and garlic
Asparagus and Lemon Pepper Vinaigrette, 50–51
Balsamic Basil, 15
Beer, Kale, and Crouton Mash-Up, The 64
Broccoli Alfredo, 69
Crème Fraîche with Apple and Cucumber, 30–31
Mediterranean, The 27
Mini-Eggplant Sliders, 96–97
Pistachio and Beets, 18–19
Pizza Volcano, The 86
Ramen, The 62–63
Roasted Brussels Sprouts with Cheddar, 29
Savory Waffle, The 78–79
Scrambled Spanakopita, The 84–85
Spicy Dubliner, The 94–95
Tillamook Cheddar and Baby Bok Choy, 43
Updated Caprese, The 24–25
Veggies and Dip, 56
Wedgie, The 65

Waffles
Dessert Waffles, 128
Savory Waffle, The 78–79
Walnut Pomegranate, 113
Wedgie, The 65
White Wine and Mushrooms, 37

About the Author

Shane (Sanford) Kearns is the blogger behind GrilledShane.com, one of the most visible grilled cheese blogs on the web! After graduating from the University of Cincinnati with a degree in Digital Design, Shane put his skills in layout and food photography to use by documenting his cooking adventures on his site, which is dedicated to elevating the awesome grilled cheese beyond mere white bread and American cheese slices. Shane lives in Solon, Ohio.